MW00896148

ELEVATING YOUR POTENTIAL

A GUIDE FOR STUDENT ATHLETES
TRANSITIONING TO COLLEGIATE SPORTS

JEREMIAH GAINES

ELEVATE TO ELEVATE

Elevating Your Potential: A Guide for Student Athletes Transitioning to Collegiate Sports

Copyright © 2020 by Jeremiah Gaines
All rights reserved.

This book or any portion thereof may not be reproduced or used in any manner whatsoever without the express written permission of the publisher except for the use of brief quotations in a book review.

Editing and typesetting by Rooted in Writing

First Printing, 2020
Elevate to Elevate LLC
www.ElevatetoElevateLLC.com

ISBN print: 978-1-7348535-0-6
ISBN e-book: 978-1-7348535-1-3

I want to dedicate this to all high school student athletes in the past that found a way to make the most of their college experiences with or without adequate guidance. I truly admire your tenacity and perseverance. Keep setting a good example. Younger athletes are watching.

To the current high school student athlete who's grinding to make their dreams and vision become a reality: I truly admire your focus and determination. Keep working on and off the field. You are learning valuable lessons that will pay off in one way or another in life.

To the future high school student athlete watching your parents, siblings, favorite player on TV, or older friends playing sports: I truly admire that you think anything is impossible. Keep this mindset, because as you get older, fears can block you from achieving your goals. Don't be afraid!

To the coaches, teachers, administrators, guardians, and community members who have impacted a student athlete: I truly thank you for taking a leap of faith and investing in the next generation of athletes. Your time, finances, conversations, and wisdom are not overlooked nor taken for granted. On behalf of all student athletes, we say thank you!

CONTENTS

INTRODUCTION

Throughout my high school journey, I had people in my life who provided valuable advice to ease my transition to college. However, I realized that I hardly used the advice because either I hadn't listened well, didn't understand what I was being told, or had completely forgotten what was said.

I did an experiment while writing this book. I researched and looked at every class that came into my university while I was a student there. The unfortunate reality was that out of five recruiting classes, there was only one class that had over 50 percent of its student athletes graduate while still on the team. (That class was around 55 percent.) But there's an even more concerning thing. I spoke with various high school coaches while writing this book, and the overwhelming majority of coaches don't think student athletes are prepared for college, especially academically and socially.

One coach said, "Most of the time, student athletes put all of their efforts into getting the chance to 'make it,' but then once they're actually there, they're not prepared for it. Then the opportunity is gone before they even realize what happened." Wow! I think student athletes simply don't know what to expect.

They don't know what they don't know.

I want to change that. The students in my study didn't complete for various reasons, but I believe this book can close the gap and help student athletes be more prepared. I want to give high school student athletes a blueprint to being successful in college.

My brother is a collegiate basketball player. While he was beginning his collegiate journey, I thought about how writing a book could give me the opportunity to tell him everything I didn't know how to say. For the first time, my purpose for writing was tangible and felt real to me. As a result, my motivation to finish this book grew.

Then my thoughts went a little deeper, and I began to realize that not only could I assist my brother, but this could give me an opportunity to be a brother, uncle, or even father figure to other student athletes who want to pursue their collegiate dreams. I now saw myself as a guide to student athletes I might not meet.

At the time of this writing, my wife and I do not have children, but we pray that we'll have children in the near future. Furthermore, we would love for our children to be great student athletes. Regardless of whether I am physically here to see my children transition to college or not, this book will be available to guide them through the process. This book is bigger than I am, and I have no choice but to pour my heart into its creation because it has a purpose.

FIND YOUR PURPOSE

I bring all this up to say that some of you have no choice but to go to college, some of you depend on college to get out of your current situation, and some of you might be hesitant about attending college. Regardless of where you're at, the most important decision you can make is your purpose for attending college. So many people are in college because it's a "good idea" or because you're expected to go. This attitude will only get you so far.

Similar to my purpose for writing this book, you must have a strong purpose for going to college and understand what perspective you're taking with you. Once my purpose was big enough, it helped me make decisions regarding what chapters to keep. It drove me during those days I didn't want to write. And it made me think that once I finished the book, I must do everything in my power to get it to as many student athletes as possible.

The same can be true for you.

Your purpose for college will help you determine where to attend, how to make decisions while you're there, what makes a good friend, and will drive you to success!

I have experienced hundreds of high school student athletes transitioning to collegiate athletics who think they are equipped and ready for success, only to realize that they are underprepared. The unfortunate reality is that they don't know they are underprepared until they are on a college campus and it's too late. They're underprepared because every person or organization may be stretched too thin.

We can't expect high schools to have an individualized method for student athletes because they have so many other competing priorities and have a very limited number of resources. Coaches are focused on winning games and teaching classes, so they have limited time to go in-depth about the college transition. Lastly, the parents either have no idea what to tell their children because they have never experienced collegiate athletics, or they are busy working a job(s) and taking care of multiple children.

There are a select group of student athletes who have the opportunity to receive this knowledge from a different source, which is amazing. However, I still think there is value in this book for that group because there are certain chapters that will force them to reflect and think about why they are choosing college and how they can maximize their financial resources while in school.

When I read a book, I consider the source. I want to know why I should listen to the author (or read what they have to say). I think it is important for the author to have some type of credentials or extensive research in a particular area.

I wrote this book based on my four years as a high school student athlete who was fortunate enough to experience the recruitment of major Division 1 football programs. Afterward, I chose to attend

Southern Methodist University (SMU) in Dallas, Texas, where I lettered for four years, started for two-and-a-half years, and received my bachelor's in sport management.

By the grace of God, I was given the opportunity to pursue my master's in education leadership and worked on SMU's campus as a student manager in the housing department, mentoring and advising high school students on how to transition into college while I also worked in the SMU Athletics department. I currently serve as an instructor at SMU, where I teach incoming freshman about choices and decisions and upperclassmen on what it takes to have good physical fitness.

All of these various experiences have given me approximately eleven years of knowledge to draw from to help you, student athlete, make a successful transition to college and set you up for a great future after graduation.

PART I

PRE-COLLEGIATE

IS YOUR "WHY" DEEP ENOUGH?

In high school, I played football, basketball, and I ran track because I had a genuine love for the art of sport. To me, high school athletics is a stress-free time to enjoy playing a sport you love with friends you've known for years. Yes, there's stress while trying to receive a scholarship, but that's the end of pressure.

In college, all of that changed for me. Football became more like a business than a game I loved. I would wonder, *What happened? Why am I slowly losing my desire to play?* But while in college, I never let myself think about these questions too much or it would mess up my mind.

Despite my waning love for playing sports, for some reason I still pushed myself to work extremely hard in every workout. I even participated in extra, voluntary workouts. If another person saw my work ethic, they wouldn't have thought I had lost my love of playing sports. Thinking back, I wonder how could someone gain the strength to do something he didn't love anymore?

First, it took continual prayer. Second, I realized that I was the glue in my family. My mom and dad were divorced, and I had a little brother who was a freshman in high school. I noticed that the only time all four of us were together was when they attended my games. I valued all of us being together in one space. But I also knew that if I started and played well, they would gladly come to games, but if I sat on the sideline, then their motivation to come would slowly disappear. The reason I pushed myself so hard was because I had a "why": a purpose that was bigger, deeper, and meant more to me than my dislike of playing sports.

I also understood that if I quit, there were several consequences I couldn't live with: I would be setting a terrible example for my brother who would go on to play collegiate sports, I couldn't leave without receiving a degree, and I couldn't set a precedent for my future family to quit when times were tough.

Why am I saying all this? Because in order for you to maximize your potential—not only in college but also in life—you need to be honest and decide your "why". Nothing else in this book will matter if you don't understand your purpose for attending college.

Purpose gives you direction.

Purpose gives you meaning.

Purpose gives you energy and wakes you up in the morning.

Purpose makes your life less stressful.

Purpose is the answer to many questions.

You need a purpose for everything you do, including college. Some of you have a dream of making it as professionals in your sport, while others want a bachelor's degree. Some of you have a grandmother you care deeply about that constantly told you to get an education, while some of you have a family business waiting for you once you graduate from college. The possible purpose for you reading can be anything. I just need you to understand your purpose and embrace it.

UNDERSTAND YOUR PURPOSE FOR ATTENDING COLLEGE

Your answer to this question has the potential to make or break the next 4–8 years of your life. Your answer will determine what college you choose, what major you choose, what people you're going to meet, the relationship you will have with your family, and so much more. Your college decision has major implications for your future, so you must be honest with yourself when answering the question: Why do you want to attend college?

There are three different mindsets we are going to explore in this chapter. These mindsets will speak to the vast majority of student athletes. The following mindsets will explain a few of the positives and negatives behind your possible way of thinking to encourage you to evaluate and/or re-evaluate your current mindset. Additionally, there are tips at the end of each mindset to help you succeed.

THE TWO-WAY PLAYER MINDSET

In sports, every coach loves a player that can do multiple skills at an above-average level. For instance, offensive football coaches love a running back that can run, catch, and block; volleyball coaches love liberos; baseball coaches love players who have all five tools; the best UFC fighters can strike and wrestle . . . the list continues for every sport. The interesting thing about players with multiple skillsets is that there is one position they prefer or consider their primary position, which means that over the course of competition, there is one position they play full time and other positions they play in short spurts.

The **two-way player mindset** is a high school athlete who wants to play collegiate sports (because they love playing or have been receiving interest from universities) but whose first priority in college will be their education.

If this is your mindset, you believe that the education you receive will give you a jump-start to your career after college. You understand that receiving a college degree separates you from other people. Or maybe you're being pushed to pursue an education by a family member or friend. As a result of having this mindset, you are saying that the driving force of your college decision will be centered around factors outside of athletics. With this thought process, you can begin to plan out your college experience to ensure you are receiving the exact information you need to realize your post-athletics dreams.

There are a few helpful tips that can help you in your journey with this mindset, but first, let's take a look at some of the advantages and disadvantages of this mindset.

Advantages

1. You understand that your time as a student athlete is limited and that you have time to set up your post-career plans early. This will make you feel as though you have a purpose and plan for attending college and not simply attending because you don't have a choice.
2. You have an edge over other student athletes because you are prioritizing your education, which means you are naturally thinking about your career. Many student athletes wait until their senior year is almost over before considering their careers.
3. You can begin establishing connections early with people on your campus that could help you find jobs and internships.
4. You can think about attending a college that has your exact major or a related organization or extracurricular activity so you can experience joy and happiness throughout your college life. By studying a major you are passionate about, you increase the chances of finding or creating a job that you love instead of one that you tolerate. Additionally, by participating in extracurricular activities you love, you maximize your social life.

Disadvantages

1. The hardest part for student athletes with this mindset is

balancing their obligations as a student and athlete while also having a meaningful social life and positioning themselves for a post-college career.

2. There is a chance you may feel isolated because only a select few student athletes may take their education seriously, especially as freshmen and sophomores.

3. You have to learn how to operate tired because coaches are going to push you physically every workout, and once that is over, you have to push yourself academically and socially.

Hopefully the disadvantages did not scare you away, because this mindset has the highest success rate for helping student athletes elevate their personal and family brands—that is, to elevate and strengthen the family name and reputation. Less than half of the US population holds a bachelor's degree, which means you can position yourself ahead of other individuals competing for similar jobs.

If this mindset still interests you, then you may be wondering what the next steps are for properly preparing for college. Take a look at these tips to help guide your thinking.

Take Time to Think about What You Want to Do for a Career.

This does not mean you need to have the rest of your life figured out, but it would help if you knew what careers interest you. As I mentioned earlier, this will help narrow your college selection down to only the schools that have your course of study or can give you the information needed to be successful after college.

Consider Where Athletics Falls on Your Priority List.

This is huge, because many student athletes choose to join sports teams at big universities as a walk-on and take student loans. There is nothing wrong with walking on, but it does become an issue if you say your mindset is education over athletics and smaller universities are offering you scholarship money to play but you do not accept it.

The total student loan debt in America is $1.45 trillion. On average, most students have to pay $37,000 in student loans after graduation. That is a steep bill to pay, especially when you choose to walk-on somewhere instead of taking the money another school is offering you. The less you have to pay for college, the better. Not only do student loans gain interest every day, but if you do not pay them in your lifetime, then your family will have to pay for them. It does not go away.

If Responsible and Able, Consider Moving Away from Family to Attend College.

If you have decided you are ready to move away, then take a leap of faith! If not, then there is no shame in staying close to home. Often, student athletes enjoy the idea of moving away from home but either aren't able to handle the freedom or didn't realize how much seeing their families meant to them. In the end, most transfer to a university close to home. You should skip the middle step and attend the close-to-home university right out of high school.[1]

Remember, be real with yourself!

THE SPECIALIST MINDSET

In sports, a specialist is important because they are often role players. This is a player that has very little interest in becoming great in multiple areas, but they have one phenomenal area in which they dominate. In basketball, you have the shooting specialist who specializes in the three-point shot. A gymnast may have a specialty on the balance beam, while goalies in hockey specialize in blocking goals. These specialists wholeheartedly believe that their one particular area is their edge over the competition.

Translating this to our mindset, a student athlete with a **specialist**

mindset wants to attend college because they want to be a professional athlete. Most student athletes who attend D-1, D-1AA, or D-2 universities and play one of the four major collegiate sports (football, basketball, soccer, and baseball) initially join because of their dreams of playing professionally. By choosing this path, you are saying that the driving force of your college decision will be athletics.

A student athlete with this mindset not only fantasizes about playing in big stadiums and arenas, but he or she is only attending college classes because of the requirement. There is nothing wrong with this mindset. Why would you not want to be the best in an area and potentially make money? Additionally, you might experience fame and popularity throughout your high school and college years, which will boost your self-confidence.

With this in mind, let's take a look at the advantages and disadvantages of this mindset.

Advantages

1. You will have one focus throughout your whole time in college, which is to improve athletically, and that could give you an edge on the playing surface.
2. Chances are, your coaches will love your intense passion for your sport because you share similar mindsets. They already spend time away from their families to invest in you as an athlete, so when an athlete has the same drive for the sport as they do, coaches love it.

Disadvantages

1. Although your singular focus is athletics, you are still required to pass a certain amount of your classes every semester. You are not a professional athlete yet, so academic requirements are still present.

2. You know the statistics. Only 1 percent of college athletes become professional athletes, and an even smaller percentage play for more than five years. This means that if you decide to have this mindset and do not make it or play for only a short amount of time, not only have you suddenly fallen short of your dreams but you would not be properly prepared for the workforce.

As you can see, the majority of the advantages and disadvantages are relatively short-term compared to the two-way player mindset. If you are still determined to reach and fulfill your lifelong dream of becoming a professional athlete, then take a peek at these tips to consider.

Think about the System You Are Going Into.

No matter how great of a player you are, you need to choose the right football program (or any other sports program, but we're using football here as an example) with the right system for your abilities so that you can the most effective player you can be. Picking the right system could be the difference between you playing earlier in your career or having to "redshirt." Being a redshirt is not negative, because it gives you a year to develop a more robust skillset. But if there's a system that's perfect for you, the redshirt might not be necessary.

Accurately Assess Yourself as an Athlete.

Some student athletes have dreams of playing for Oklahoma or Ohio State or Alabama, but the best thing for them might be to attend Tulane University or Vanderbilt so they can either play early or develop their skillset with limited pressure to play. The best way to improve your chances of playing professionally is to (*a*) play and have game tape, then (*b*) play well and dominate in any level you compete against.

THE LIFE PLAYER MINDSET

The **life player mindset** is the high school athlete who plays sports in high school because they enjoy the camaraderie (or because they have to play) but has no desire to attend college and wants to have a job immediately after high school graduation.

These student athletes choose other life decisions over attending college. Some student athletes who are life players are forced into this option because they need to take care of their families; some would rather make money, because most students do not make a large amount of money during college; and others do not think college is for them.

Those options are all completely acceptable, but there are some hard realities to that decision.

Even though you are not going to college, it is essential that you acquire a skillset that will make you effective in a field. As a result, you'll need to either educate yourself informally, on the job, or get a mentor to teach you.

In most cases, there are limits to how high you can climb within a company without a degree or certification. As you get older and want promotions, you might get passed over because you do not have a degree. Is it fair? Who knows . . . but it is something to think about.

Advantages

1. You have the opportunity to work more and make more money.
2. You don't have to complete weekly assignments for a grade.
3. You will not have student loan debt.

Disadvantages

1. Although you have the ability to make money sooner, individuals who earn a bachelor's degree earn almost $400 per week more than individuals with only a high school degree. (US Bureau of Labor Statistics, 2018)
2. It's harder to access self-taught learning materials, unlike colleges, which provide you with resources such as books, labs, and more.
3. College is the best place to build both social relationships and business networking opportunities. Without going, it will be more difficult for you to build these types of relationships organically.

Disclaimer

The rest of this book is targeted toward student athletes who want to pursue a college education. My intention is not to exclude anyone, but the purpose of this book is to guide to student athletes through recruitment, the college application process, and a successful college completion.

---

1. Search for school options: www.Niche.com

BEGIN WITH THE END IN MIND

I remember the first class I took in a college classroom was on July 5, 2013. It was an introductory English course, and it was a class with all student athletes: six football players and three volleyball players. All of the students in the class were nervous because we were in a new environment, with new people, learning new information. As students, we had hoped that we had received enough training at our high school and through our parents to be prepared for college, but we truly didn't know until the class started.

During class, we were tasked with reading a book and writing short papers as a response to it. Over the course of the four-week term (summer classes are short), we probably wrote between eight and twelve papers, ranging from half-a-page to ten-pages long. I wish I could tell you that all of the students in the class were able to successfully complete the course, but unfortunately, two or three students failed or dropped the course.

As I reflect on this experience, I can think of a few possibilities as to why this might have happened to these students:

1. They believed the class would be easy and didn't take it seriously.
2. They believed the coursework would be too challenging and put forth minimal effort.
3. They were not prepared and didn't have the tools to be successful, either because their high school did not prepare them or because they did not take high school seriously.

Regardless, the end result of the class for these students was not ideal. After dropping or failing the course, they did not receive any credit for the summer class and were forced to take a similar class again during the year, making their graduation date later. Additionally, they were asked to attend extra tutoring sessions to ensure they were equipped with the tools to help them succeed academically.

Although there isn't anything wrong with needing more help, my desire for you reading this chapter is to make sure that you learn the most information you can in high school before reaching a college classroom so that you are not forced to drop or fail a class.

In your off-season programs, I'm sure your coaches have said these words:

"The work you put in now will pay off during the season."

These words are very true. During the season, you don't have the time—nor does it make sense—to gain muscle and endurance. The goal is to maintain, because during the season you have to game plan and be ready for competition. The information you learn in school works the same way. The work you've put in and are putting in now is the "off-season," and your future in academics is the "season."

Most people in life live for the moment with minimal thought toward the future. Their main goal is to survive any way they can with the least amount of effort. This is especially true in school. What people fail to realize is that they might not need a class's information today, but down the line, the material may appear again. If you don't already have the information, you are going to have to learn it—usually after others have already learned it—and now you are behind. The goal of this chapter is to help you make it easier on yourself and learn the information instead of simply surviving in class.

The Information You Learn in High School Has an Impact on Your Educational Future.

If you aspire to be a collegiate athlete, do not allow your junior high and high school teachers to be a crutch for you. You need to learn the information regardless of your initial mindset, because whether you have the specialist or two-way player mindset, you still have to attend classes.

The goal is to exit college quickly and with as much information as possible, so if you take the time to invest in your education early, then you will be ahead of the game in college. If you do not, then you will eventually have to relearn the information through remedial courses that do not count toward graduation, which will extend your time in college, or you will be a student that falls behind in every class.

In order to prevent these alternatives from happening, here are a few things to assist you.

Regardless of Whether You Enjoy the Class or Not, Actually Learn the Information.

From my experience, the studying method that is used the most by high school student athletes is cramming. A large number of students wait until the night before a test to study all the materials. Often, student athletes receive a grade that they find "acceptable," so they continue using this strategy. The bad side of cramming is that two minutes after the test, they forget all the information.

The purpose of the test was to see how much information you retained so that you can carry it with you throughout your life. In order to have long-term success, you must do everything in your power to retain your classes' information because there is a strong possibility that they'll come back in college.

For example, pay attention to sentence structure in your English class. You will have to take writing classes in college, and most classes will make you write anyway, so the best thing is just to learn it early. Furthermore, jobs value individuals who have strong writing skills and can effectively write emails, grants for money, and send proposals to potential business clients.

Take 30–60 Minutes to Review the Information after Each Class.

Studies show that if you review the information you learned in class right after class, you will retain 80 percent more information than if you wait. To be honest, this seems like a very aspirational and lofty goal, but the key is that you review the information from classes shortly after they're over. The most common practice is to attend class and wait until a week before the test (or later) to review the class notes. But the sooner you can review your notes, the more likely you will learn the information long-term.

Do Not Be Afraid to Attend Tutoring or Have Study Groups.

It is a mistake to believe that tutoring is only for students who are struggling. In college, the students who have the most success are those who have a tutor or form small study groups so that they learn the material before failing becomes an issue. Tutoring and study groups serve two purposes: they give you a set time to study the material so you do not procrastinate, and they connect you with individuals who can help you understand some of the class content you're struggling with—and you can do the same for them!

START FAST, FINISH STRONG

I had never realized how important my GPA was until I was being recruited by universities. Although people tried to prepare me for the college application process, I never thought about it until I was forced to start the process. My process started when I began taking college-level courses, but outside of that, the first agenda item was taking the ACT and SAT.

If you want to attend a four-year university, the ACT and SAT are required tests that measure your readiness for college. (I do not like the tests, but they are a requirement, so I dealt with it.) I chose to take the ACT because I had heard it was easier, because if you missed a question, it wouldn't hurt your score (so if I guessed, I could still get it right).

One day, I was preparing for practice in our locker room, and I saw a sheet of paper. It had been there for a while, but it had never caught my attention until then. The paper was from the NCAA Eligibility Center. On one side it had the ACT scoring, with GPAs from 3.5 down to 2.0 on the other. These were the ACT scores you needed in order to be eligible to play college sports immediately. The higher your GPA was, the lower score you had to make on the standardized test.

I took a strong look at the scoring and found my GPA. Thankfully, my GPA was around 3.7 so I only had to score a 7 per section on the ACT. Later, I learned that there's a scoring scale because some people do very well in school but have test anxiety and do terrible on tests, and the NCAA does not want to penalize your four years of high school for one test.

Obviously, I was happy that my score didn't have to be as high to be eligible. I didn't want to take the test in the first place. I was very thankful that although I hadn't thought about the process before, I had taken my education and GPA seriously enough to make it easier on myself when it came to taking the ACT.

It is very important to get off to a good start in the first quarter/set/period of the game. The first quarter sets the tone for the game. If you get off to a fast start, you can have your opposition playing catch-up all night. If the reverse happens, then you could be in for a long night yourself. The same is true for your GPA. It is always easier to start fast and make great grades than to chill early and try to recover.

Getting off to a good start is amazing, but you also have to finish strong. I have seen teams start fast and build huge leads only to relax and blow the lead. If you get off to a fast start with your GPA and relax in classes, your GPA could fall just as fast. This chapter is to help you start with a great GPA and finish with a great GPA.

MAKE THE HIGHEST GRADES POSSIBLE: ESPECIALLY WHEN TAKING COLLEGE-CREDIT CLASSES

Your GPA will specifically help you with the college application process. There are two different processes student athletes have to endure: NCAA Eligibility requirements *and* applications for a specific college.

There is a section later in this book where we'll talk about the NCAA Eligibility Center and how it affects your collegiate sports future, but for now suffice it to say that the Eligibility Center is most concerned about your grades in core classes. Your core classes are math, English, science, and history. Your GPA in these classes is the set point for your ACT or SAT score on the sliding scale. As previously mentioned, the sliding scale is in place so that the higher your GPA is, the lower you have to score on one of the tests in order to be eligible to play. If you are not a good test taker, then having the sliding scale could help if you took care of your business and kept a high GPA.

This does not mean that you should neglect your other classes, because they are more important for the above second reason: getting into your dream school. When you have a dream to attend a university and play sports, you have to first be accepted into the school.

Most colleges and universities use your cumulative, or total, GPA to decide whether or not to accept you. This means that not only are the core classes important, but your other classes are added to your cumulative GPA. In order to be accepted into the school of your dreams, especially if they are highly selective, you must maintain a high GPA.

Universities use your GPA not only to accept you into school but also to determine academic scholarships. Student athletes who play sports such as swimming, diving, golf, and equestrian and are not on full-ride scholarships should work hard to increase academic scholarship money. How can we ensure you have a high GPA by graduation?

Take Advantage of Classes That Boost Your GPA.

These are classes that are easier to receive a higher grade in than others or that study topics that come naturally to you. Do not be lazy in these classes. As we've talked about before, *learn the information* and then ensure you have an A at the end of the semester.

Take Pre-AP or AP Classes.

If you enjoy a particular subject and it has a Pre-AP or AP compo-
nent, don't be afraid to take those higher-level classes. These classes
are worth substantially more points than regular classes. For
instance, if you make a "B" in an AP class, then you will receive a 4.0
—the exact same as an "A" in a regular class on your GPA. If you
make an "A" in the class, then you will receive a 5.0, which is more
than the 4.0 "A" in a regular class. This is will boost your GPA and
give you room for error in other classes that may be more difficult
for you.

Take Your Classes Seriously All throughout High School.

Another thing to remember is that colleges initially view only your
grades up until your junior year because you're applying early senior
year. This is important because you will not have the opportunity to
"make up" your grades during your senior year. This does not mean
that you should blow off your senior year—you still have to submit
your final grades as well in order to *stay* accepted at the school.

EXECUTE, EXECUTE, EXECUTE

On the surface, recruitment is easier than ever now. The invention of the internet with YouTube, Facebook, Instagram, etc. has made it easier for scouts to find good players for the programs, as opposed to waiting to visit schools or having CDs sent to their facilities. On a deeper level, because it is easier and there are more student athletes making highlight videos, college coaches are being overloaded with recruits now. In my opinion, you still have the same chances of getting recruited as you did twenty years ago, so the question is this: How do you stand out in the midst of thousands of high school athletes?

In football, if you ran the play and read it perfectly but missed the tackle, dropped the ball, or fumbled, then you didn't execute. If a pitcher in baseball threw 8 2/3 innings and gave up 0 runs, but the last batter hit a double and the pitcher's team lost, then he didn't execute. If a basketball player successfully crossed a defender but missed the layup, she didn't execute. If a volleyball team was down two sets, came roaring back, and lost 15–13 in the final set, then they didn't execute. All of these examples show that no matter how hard you try and compete, you must execute or else you don't get the results you want.

Execution is the key to any person's dream. Many people have great ideas. Many people start building their ideas. Many people work hard. But, very few people actually execute to a level that sees their dreams come true. The purpose of this chapter is to provide you with simple, tangible steps that will help you execute and realize your dream of being a collegiate athlete.

"HOW DO I GET RECRUITED?"
AN ATHLETE'S PERSPECTIVE

The recruiting process is different for everyone. Depending on the amount of attention you are getting from schools and if you are receiving the attention you think is appropriate for your talent level, your experience could be different. Some athletes love the recruitment process because they have college coaches coming to their high schools and houses, and they enjoy the attention they're receiving.

Some people receive attention but do not enjoy it because all they want to do is play their sport and attend school at the next level. Others have a very unpleasant experience because they believe they're good enough to be at a certain level, but they're not receiving the attention that they believe they deserve.

So the question is: How do you actually catch the attention of college scouts?

There is no guarantee that these tips will make you a D-1 collegiate athlete, not at all. But I wanted to give you some tips on the process from a collegiate athlete's perspective.

Get on the Varsity Team.

The first one is relatively obvious, but make sure you are performing well in high school practices to ensure you play on the varsity team. If you do not play on varsity, it is nearly impossible to gain recruiting momentum.

Maximize Your Measurables.

Your "measurables" are what separate you from the rest of the competition before you even start the game. They are God-given physical attributes that are oftentimes your advantages over the competition. You have very little control over your measurables. Take speed, for example. You can definitely work on your speed and get faster, but your genetics either limit or enhance your likelihood of being fast. Other measurables include height, weight, and overall athletic ability.

Fair or unfair, coaches often recruit based on potential, not ability. If you have the right measurables, coaches feel they can teach you other techniques and the nuances of your sport regardless of your current skill level. If you have great measurables, do not use this as an opportunity to be lazy. Maximize your measurables by complementing them with the following two ways to get recruited. If you do not have great measurables, don't worry; these next two steps are still achievable.

Dominate the Competition.

Your ability to play the game and execute your various techniques is probably the biggest and best way to catch the attention of a scout. One former Division I coach said that when he would go to a game or watch a film, he'd measure whether someone was a Division I athlete or not by asking, "Is this individual dominating the competition two out of every three plays?" This may vary depending on the type of competition you're playing, but ultimately, are you playing your sport at a high level?

Outside of having amazing measurables, dominating the competition means developing a unique skillset. If you are a golfer, work on your putts. If you are a wrestler, master takedowns. If you are a sprinter, work on your start. In each sport, there are endless skills you can master. All it takes is you putting in the hours for individual skills development before and after practice and in the off-season.

Skills extend beyond physical ability into your mental ability. Do you understand the sport you are playing at a higher level than your peers? Do you watch film of yourself and the opposition? Are you able to perform when it's a close game? Can your coach trust you to remain poised if the opposing team is talking trash? These are all important questions that you and your coach must say yes to when college scouts come to visit.

Effort, Effort, Effort

This last one is all about effort, effort, effort. To be completely honest, this is probably something that coaches look at last, but there have been exceptions to the rule. There have been times when coaches travel to watch a particular player, and as the game progresses, they spot another player who is undersized and not very skilled but is running all around the playing surface. That energy and effort is contagious! Put in the extra effort, and you never know what can happen.

THE IN-BETWEEN PHASE

One day during my freshman year of high school, I walked into our school field house in our athletic facility. It was tradition for our head coach to stand outside with letters in his hand. Those letters were from universities to student athletes at our school. I was thrilled when my coach handed me my first letter—and it was from the University of Oregon, no less.

At the time, I just knew I was destined to talk to Oregon coaches and take a trip up to Eugene for a visit. This was right at the beginning of Oregon being the standard for trendy uniforms, so every athlete—especially football players—wanted to go there. Oregon was the first university to send a coach to look at me in high school, so this gave me even more confidence that they would heavily recruit me. Unfortunately, I never talked to Oregon again, and I never received a scholarship.

Thankfully, Oregon had not been the only school interested in me, but I talk about my Oregon situation now because the in-between phase can be a little confusing. You may feel a school has heavy interest in you playing for them, but then all of sudden they cut off communication or take forever to offer you a scholarship—or never offer the scholarship.

At my high school (I am sure it happens other places), athletes often take the letters they receive and publicly say that major programs are recruiting them. Sometimes that is the case, but as the recruiting process continues, these students either walk-on or go to a very small school, and you wonder, *What happened?* Well, that's the in-between phase for you.

Let's find out how to operate during this period.

Have you ever been on a team that wasn't a bad team, but they weren't good either? On any night you could win, but you could also lose if you didn't play well. This in-between stage in recruitment could have you feeling the same way.

When you are in between an object or a group of people (or really anything), you feel very awkward. I mean, you've worked on your skills, gave effort, worked on your measurables, and you're receiving some attention but no scholarships. You may feel confused about where you truly are in this world of recruiting. Those feelings perfectly fine and normal. This chapter is here to help you govern yourself through this period.

WHAT HAPPENS BETWEEN RECEIVING LETTERS AND THE SCHOLARSHIP?

There is an in-between phase before official recruitment where you might be receiving attention from colleges, but college coaches are not contacting you directly. You may attend various camps to get exposure to college campuses, or you may even go on unofficial visits to campus. To be clear, any high school student athlete can attend an unofficial visit, and coaches may give a campus tour, but this still does not mean you are being recruited by those schools.

During my process, I didn't think I was being recruited by a school until I was offered a scholarship or talked to a school multiple times either in person or over the phone. There is no timetable for how long this period may last; it differs for all players. Regardless, there are still a few tips to help with this awkward time.

Always Have a Great Attitude toward Your Coaches and Be the Best Version of Yourself.

This is especially important during the recruitment process because you do not want to raise red flags to coaches. You never know what day a particular college coach will come to your school, and it is embarrassing to do punishment runs or be on suspension when a coach visits. In the beginning, you have no idea how many colleges will recruit you, and if you make a bad first impression, you might have significantly hindered your chances to play on a particular level.

Coaches talk to other coaches, and word spreads fast about a player's character—both good and bad. This is not the time to be a bad teammate (there is never a time, might I add) or talk back to your coaches, or get into an argument with a teacher or principal, or post inappropriate content on social media, or get involved with the police. College coaches truly do their homework before they choose to offer scholarships. Money is not unlimited, so in order for them to receive a return on their investment in you, they must make sure they are recruiting a player who has the integrity to not only enroll at the university but also graduate.

Keep Working and Getting Better!

This is not the time to relax. Once you gain a college's attention, you are going to be on the scouting report of every coach you play. You are going to have a target on your back, and other student athletes are going to try gain scholarships off of you. Use this college attention as an opportunity to work harder and show why you deserve to be receiving attention.

Fill Out Every Questionnaire That Comes to Your House, No Matter Your Interest in the School.

You don't know whether you'll be a D-1 or junior college player until you receive scholarships, and if you ignore certain colleges, you may miss opportunities to receive their scholarships. Also, the question-naire is an easy way to let a college know if you have an interest in them without directly contacting you. They'll then have updated contact information for you when it comes time to officially recruit.

Attending Camps is Beneficial, Especially the Camps Hosted by Specific Colleges.

Hundreds of athletes attend these camps, and it is hard to stand out, but you can make a difference with extreme athleticism or great technique.

Talk to the College Coach.

Don't be afraid to ask college coaches, respectfully, where you stand on their recruiting board. For example: "Hey Coach, I'm enjoying the relationship we've been establishing over these past few weeks (or months), but I was just curious about where I currently stand on your recruiting board for my position. Would you be willing to discuss that with me?" An honest coach will understand and answer. If you receive a straightforward answer, regardless of whether or not it was what you wanted to hear, you can thank them for their time. But if they are beating around the bush, then be careful. Trust your gut instincts.

THE TRANSITION OF POWER

As I began to write this chapter, I remembered two stories that I think will help demonstrate the topic. For the first one, we'll have to travel back to the spring of my junior year.

Praise the Lord, my recruitment had started to pick up. Coaches usually came during fifth period, athletics period, to watch us work-out. On this particular day, we had two universities visit the school. Coincidently, this was the same day our coach would read off the names of players who were currently not doing well on their progress reports in class, and these students would then have to complete punishment runs.

At the time I was struggling with a Pre-AP Pre-Calculus, and I was one of the athletes that had to do punishment runs. As you can imagine, this was extremely embarrassing. On top of it, *two* college coaches were there, so of course that was not the best first impression to make.

After completing the runs, one of the coaches had a conversation with me, encouraging me to improve in the classroom. Thankfully, it didn't negatively impact my recruitment, but they easily could've changed their minds and stopped recruiting me.

The second story is a little more personal. There was a particular university who offered me my first scholarship. I was close to verbally committing to this university several times, but something kept stopping me. Every time I was around the coaches, it felt like they were trying to bully me into committing to their school. If you ask anyone who knows me, they'll say I am very stubborn and will do the exact opposite of the thing you are attempting to bully me into. After a few months, the coaching staff made me choose.

The coach recruiting me called one day and said in a very calm voice, "If you do not make a decision by Friday, then we are going to have to move on in our recruitment to someone else."

This statement initially caught me off guard, but then I realized I wouldn't attend that institution because I did not want to rush a decision that would have major implications for the rest of my life. Yes, I could have committed and then decommitted later if another school offered a scholarship, but I had made a promise to myself that I would be a man of my word. If I committed to a school, then my recruitment would be over. Also, at the time I was getting recruited, the Transfer Portal didn't yet exist, so if I had transferred from the school, I would have had to sit out a whole year. Changing locations after a year was also not ideal, so at the end of the day, I did not choose to commit to that school and chose another university.

In sports, there is this big word called **momentum**. Momentum in sports, simply put, is multiple positive, big moments that are working in your favor. Every team wants momentum on their side, because with it your team and fans gain more confidence and control. If you are controlling the game and are confident 99 percent of the time, you'll win.

Do not be mistaken: *keeping* momentum is just as important as *getting* momentum. You can lose momentum very quickly by trying a trick play or making a bad substitution at the wrong time, creating negative plays that will swing the momentum to the other side.

In the beginning of the recruiting process, you are working really hard to gain the attention of coaches, and they have the authority to reject or decline recruiting you. You are trying to gain momentum. When you start receiving scholarship(s), you now have the momentum, control, and confidence. If you abuse this privilege of having momentum in recruitment, you can easily lose it through bad mistakes and decisions. This chapter is to help you keep momentum and use this momentum to help you win the recruitment game.

The goal: choosing the right university for you!

WHAT HAPPENS WHEN SCHOLARSHIPS START COMING IN?

Finally! Coaches are communicating with you often, scholarship offers are present, and you are attracting the attention you desperately desired. What happens now? Once you start receiving scholarship opportunities, you begin to have a small amount of control. Universities are attempting to prove to you why their programs and schools are the best fit for you. This is typically the best part for most student athletes, because your dream of becoming a collegiate athlete is beginning to come true—but this opportunity does come with its challenges. Here are a few tips that might help you through the process.

Be Careful and Bold!

Do not let the smooth-talking coach or fancy campus distract you from your goals. Do not be afraid to ask questions about your well-being. Here is a list of things to consider:

1) **The official visit.** For most student athletes, the best part of the recruiting process—besides receiving scholarship offers—is the official visit. An official visit is the university's best pitch to a student athlete they want to attend their school. Official visits are from Friday night until Sunday afternoon. Universities fly student athletes in from across the country to speak with coaches, advisors, counselors, and major fans of the program.

You also receive free meals, attend various sporting events, and have an opportunity to speak with members of the team. You will be given a "host" that is selected by the coaches to show you a good time.

Ask current players their opinion on the coach and program. Make sure that you take advantage of this time with the team members, because they will give you a glimpse into the reality of playing for that program. Try to talk with team members who are not hosts, because they could possibly offer a different perspective. Hosts are often selected because they are the best representation of the program, but you want to know the other side as well. If both sides are the same, that is amazing. If they are not, well, don't let this information steer you in one way or another, but keep it in the back of your mind.

2) Available majors. Ask the academic advisor on their thoughts about allowing you to take hard majors (like engineering or business) while playing your sport. Some of my teammates wanted to pursue "hard" majors but were asked not to because an academic advisor's first priority is to keep you eligible.

3) Alumni life. Think about how important a connection to the alumni base is to the program. Texas A&M has one of the best alumni bases because they truly believe that once you receive your Aggie ring, you are part of the family. This is important because these A&M ties can help you receive internships, jobs, mentorships, and other resources vital to your success.

Continue to Make Good Decisions in Regard to Your Behavior.

When you are active on social media, don't post anything that you don't want college coaches to see. (That's a tip for life, not just recruitment.) Don't get in trouble with the law. Treat people and yourself with respect and you'll be fine.

Never Feel Pressured to Make a Decision before You Are Ready.

Your college decision, as we discussed earlier, will impact your life for a long time. Coaches want you to come to their universities, but do not let them dictate your decision. Take your time during the process. Some coaches might say "you have until this date or that date to make a decision" or "we will move on if you don't commit." They are perfectly within their rights to say that, and if you feel comfortable committing to their university, then make that decision with conviction. But if you need more time, take the time!

Remember, they want you, and you are in the driver's seat. There might be a slight risk that the school takes the scholarship away from you, and if that happens, they didn't want you as badly as you thought anyway. You are in control. Also, there could be pressure to commit to a particular university from your family and other people in the community where there are mutual feelings of love and respect. Those feelings are valid and should be there, but you can't let them cloud your judgment. At the end of the day, it is your journey, and when it gets tough, you are actually the one going through it, not them!

Later in the book, there is a chapter on mentors that may be beneficial to assist you during the recruiting process.

Develop, or Maintain, a Spirit of Humility.

Through the process, don't become entitled, mistreat others, or expect people to know who you are and give you items and food for free. It is important to remember that humility is what got you to where you are. That humility kept you hungry in your sport, made you selfless, and shaped you into a nice person worth approaching to have a conversation with. Every athlete who is prideful and selfish eventually falls from their pedestal and realizes they are human as well. Don't make a situation humble you—continue to keep yourself humble by helping others on and off the field.

There Is Nothing Wrong with Attending a Junior College.

There is a misconception that junior college is terrible, but there are three major reasons why some people should attend junior college:

1. You have more time to develop your skills with less pressure.
2. You have a better opportunity to attend a better university. Universities always look for top-tier transfers because they want players with experience.
3. You can prepare yourself academically.

You Only Need One School to Like You.

Yes, it sounds sexy to have twenty, thirty, or forty schools fighting over your decision, but the reality is that you are one person who can only attend one school. So whether you have one offer or many offers, you should rejoice in the fact that you are wanted and someone values you. In my opinion, marriage is at its best when you marry one person. You don't need every person in the world to love you, just one! The exact same is true for the recruiting process. As long as you have one school that believes in you and your ability, then that is all you need to play on the next level.

THE MIDDLEMEN

It's not a straight shot to get into a collegiate sports program; you first have to pass some gatekeepers, or middlemen, before your decision is final. Think of these middlemen as the referees. The object in most sports is to beat the opposition: the other team. While your main focus is to beat that other team, there are referees in place to ensure that both sides are playing according to the rules and to keep players safe. This chapter will take a look into first the college application process—because you are a *student* athlete that attends a university— and then the NCAA Eligibility Center, which ensures you play according to various NCAA rules.

COLLEGE APPLICATION

We've discussed two different aspects of the college application, your GPA and the ACT/SAT, but there's more that you need to prepare for. The college application was a part of the process that I didn't think about until it was time to complete it. Let me repeat this: *just because you receive a scholarship offer from a university doesn't mean that you are accepted into that school.*

Some universities tend to allow student athletes who are slightly under their academic standards to attend the university, but others keep their standards high. For example, Stanford University is a highly selective university that only accepts the best students across the country. If you have a 2.7 GPA and average scores, your chances of attending Stanford are slim—but other schools may accept you.

The application process does take time, but it is definitely doable. Thankfully, at the university I chose, we had a director of football operations that kept us on a timeline to complete our applications. Hopefully your director does the same, but if not, here's what you need to do.

Rank Your Priorities.

This is the time when you go back to Chapter 1 and decide whether you are approaching college with a two-way player or specialist mindset.

1. **Two-way player mindset:** distance from home, degree program(s), organizations, alumni connections, connection to jobs/internships, size of campus, teacher/student ratio*, and academic success resources (writing labs, tutoring, learning disability assistance).
2. **Specialist mindset:** coaching scheme, number of players in your position, and classification of players in your position (i.e. sophomores, seniors).

The rest of the chapter is academic. Regardless of your mindset, I want you to focus academically.

Create Your Personal Student Profile.

Simply review your transcript to see your rank, GPA, and ACT/SAT scores.

Select Your Top Schools Based on Your Student Profile.

Regardless of your recruitment, think about your schools beyond their sports programs. Most importantly, does the school have your proposed major?

SMU Upward Bound, a program that equips students with resources to succeed in pre-collegiate performance and make their higher education pursuits achievable, recommends using this process for school selection:

1. Pick two "reach" schools (your dream schools).
2. Pick two "match" schools (where you have a better chance of getting accepted).
3. Pick one "safe" school (where you qualify for automatic admittance).

This process helps so that you aren't applying to a hundred schools—because that's a lot of work.

Review the Admission Process for Each School.

Visit the website for each school and research the admission process, because each school's system could be different.

Collect Documents for Each School.

Most colleges request at minimum your transcripts, letters of recommendation, a photo ID, and ACT/SAT scores.

Pay Attention to Essay Questions.

Write your essays according to the rules established for each school and continually get them revised. English teachers and other members at each athlete's high school will gladly assist you.

Submit and Select.

Complete the application for each school, have it reviewed, and then submit! Once you are accepted and have received your financial awards, ensure that you understand the ramifications of their scholarship eligibility.

THE NCAA ELIGIBILITY CENTER

The purpose of this section is to briefly go over a resource that every athlete hoping to play on Division 1 and 2 teams will have to register through: the NCAA Eligibility Center[1].

The NCAA Eligibility Center is the section of the NCAA that ensures all Division 1 and 2 athletes are academically eligible and maintain amateur status prior to and throughout their time in college[2]. This center is not associated with any particular university, nor will it help you find the right college. The sole purpose is to make sure that you are eligible to participate in sports.

It is impossible to include all the information needed for the NCAA Eligibility Center, but I will highlight the major points. Here's a timeline of what you need to do through high school.

Freshman Year

At the beginning of your freshman year, find out the NCAA core courses at your high school. Core courses are the most important academic requirement because the NCAA only looks at those courses for eligibility requirements. You have to complete ten core courses by the end of your junior year and sixteen by graduation. Core courses include a combination of English, math, physical science, social sciences, and a few others (exact details below).

After viewing the core course sheet, create a four-year plan that ensures you successfully fulfill the requirements. Preparing ahead of time will also give you the opportunity to create a schedule that gives you a manageable load. For example, if math is an area of improvement for you, you can take your harder math classes in the off-season or when you have a lighter load so that you can focus more on math.

At some point during freshman year, you should make a NCAA profile account. They say that you should set aside fifteen to twenty minutes to complete the initial registration. I know this is early—most student athletes are not receiving heavy interest yet—but if you complete this step early, you won't have to worry about it later when you have to complete other applications, tests, and essays.

Sophomore Year

During your sophomore year, you should do two things. The first is to review your progress from your freshman year and ensure you are on the right track to completing those core course requirements. The second is to take a practice standardize test (i.e., PSAT) so that you can become familiar with it before taking it at some point your junior year.

Junior Year

During junior year, you should create a NCAA Certification Account (it makes you certified to play in college). It cost $90 for US and Canadian athletes but $150 for international athletes. Send a transcript to the Eligibility Center at the end of the year.

Also, similar to sophomore year, review your progress toward completing the academic core requirements, but make sure that you have reached the ten hours of core credits.

Last, take your first ACT and/or SAT test so that if you receive an unsatisfactory score, you have plenty of time to take the test again. If you are not satisfied, do not be afraid to reach out to programs that offer ACT and SAT preparation. If you are satisfied with your scores, you can send them to the NCAA and universities. (You'll need to research the universities' school codes.)

Senior Year

During senior year, you should take the ACT or SAT again if need be. There is an amateurism questionnaire you should fill out in your NCAA account. Review your transcripts again to ensure you are on track to meet academic core requirements. At the end of your senior year, make sure you send your final transcripts to NCAA Eligibility Center.

Remember, this list is not comprehensive, so please refer to the website and call a NCAA Eligibility Center representative to receive full instructions.

---

1. NCAA Eligibility Center: https://web3.ncaa.org/ecwr3/
2. NCAA academic requirements:
   http://www.ncaa.org/student-athletes/future/test-scores

PART II

PREPPING YOUR MINDSET
FOR COLLEGE

TRANSFER PORTAL

I went back and forth on whether to add a chapter on the Transfer Portal or not, because it primarily impacts D-1 athletes, but I think it's important for me to mention it since it's so prevalent in the media. I think it's important to start the preparation phase for college with the portal because I think it's important to know that you have liberties and freedoms that weren't always available—but, to be transparent, I hope you never use it.

When I was being recruited in 2012, there wasn't a Transfer Portal. That means if D-1 student athletes decided to transfer to other D-1 schools, then we were forced to sit out a year, except for extreme circumstances. We always thought that rule was nonsense, because coaches could hop from university to university every year but we had to lose a year of eligibility. As a result, I'm glad you have the option, but let's think of this option like a trick play, set, or shot in your sport.

Most of you are familiar with trick plays. Trick plays are plays that are specifically designed by coaches to create a big play or opportunity that's completely different from what your team usually does. It throws the other team off guard. When you use the trick play, you have to execute the play perfectly. Once you use it one time, the play is on film and every team will see it and be ready—which means it probably won't work again. You only get once.

The interesting thing about trick plays is that you might practice a trick play all year and never use it. Coaches would much rather run their base or simple offense every game rather than rely on trick plays to beat the opponent. The Transfer Portal works the same way. Your family, your friends, your supporters, and I would much rather you make the correct college decision the first time than transfer. We definitely don't want you going into your new situation thinking you can easily transfer. Transferring brings a lot of paperwork, moving, building new relationships, answering questions about why you left . . . It's a hassle.

WHEN YOU DO TRANSFER

To this point, I've only referenced negative aspects, but there are certain circumstances that might push you to transfer. I am not going to tell you when or why to transfer, but I will inform you on a few guidelines.

If you do decide to transfer, then I wanted to offer list of boundaries with the portal. (All of these boundaries are true if you are academically eligible at your current school and stay eligible at your future school.)

1. For many years, student athletes had the ability to transfer to other universities and be eligible immediately, but they had to be a graduate of a university, graduate transfer, or transfer to a smaller university (i.e., D-1 athlete transferring to D-2). With the Transfer Portal, you now have the opportunity for a *one-time transfer* exception (your trick play).

2. Student athletes have to be released from the previous school.

3. You must complete a waiver and submit it to the NCAA.
4. If a student athlete wants to transfer due to disciplinary suspension, he/she does not qualify.
5. For more information, check www.NCAA.org.

COMPETE IN EVERY ASPECT OF LIFE

During my senior year in college, I was working a part-time job on campus in the housing department. One day toward the end of the semester, I was doing my usual tasks, and a freshman from the football team walked into the office. I walked up and spoke to him, and then I left so he could handle his business. Every time a player came in, I would always wonder why they needed assistance, but I never thought much about it. Approximately two months later, I was talking to another one of my former teammates, and somehow the same player that came to the office came up in the conversation. Come to find out, this particular player failed the majority of his classes and was no longer a part of the team. I was astonished and then realized everything made sense now . . .

Competition brings the best out of all of us. Competition has a way of challenging us internally in order to successfully complete a task at our highest level possible. There's competition everywhere: high school class rank, sports, business, sibling rivalries, first in line in the cafeteria. Literally, it's everywhere. I would venture to say that athletes are the best at competing. Even the least competitive athlete is way more competitive than your average person. Unfortunately, there is one area in some student athletes' lives they don't compete well in. The STUDENT part of STUDENT athlete. This chapter is for those high school student athletes that love competition in their sport but didn't compete as a student in high school. I want you to learn so you don't end up being sent home for poor grades.

You are smart enough to succeed in a college classroom.

"This school thing is not for me." "I am not smart enough for that class or college." "I am just here to play sports." These are just a few of the statements some student athletes say regularly. You might be one of those athletes.

There is a great proverb in the Bible that is amazing. It says, "For as a man thinks in his heart, so is he." (Proverbs 23:7) This means that whatever you think or say about yourself is true. If you say negative things about yourself and school, then you will find that your grades will suffer. On the other hand, if you think positive, greatness can happen. You are not a dumb jock! There is no such thing.

Very few people are smart enough to memorize a playbook, strong enough to push their body to the max during practices and workouts, and able to incorporate both the mental and physical aspects of the sport at the same time to make a great play. The best athletes outwork everyone on the playing surface. I believe part of the reason they work so hard is because they desire to be the best, but I think there's another reason as well.

Athletes are accustomed to success on the field, and when they fail it is broadcasted for fans, players, and coaches to see. As a result, athletes work tirelessly to decrease the chances of this potential failure. The problem is while athletes are in school, there is a lack of desire to compete in the classroom.

Often, I have seen the best athletes quit or simply show a lack of effort so they have an excuse. Maybe they're scared to fail if they put forth effort. These students don't realize that if they transfer the energy used in their sports to the classroom, they would experience similar results.

How do you do this? Let's take a look.

Build Small Wins in the Classroom to Help with Your Confidence.

It is easy to forget as a high school athlete that there was a time when you were not as good in your sport. You were once a little kid who had to learn the fundamentals of the game. During this time, no matter how good you were compared to others, you still needed to make major improvements in order to be where you are today.

At that time, it did not feel as though you were trying really hard to be good. You just worked hard, and one day you looked up and realized you were good at the sport. Essentially, you made very little progress every single day and built on top of your successes.

Treat school the same way. Do not be intimidated by your teachers in high school and college or by the "smartest kid in class." All you have to do is listen in class, review your notes after class, and do every assignment every day, and you will see that you are competent and can be great in the classroom. This does not mean you will master everything quickly, but you will make progress. And that is all you need.

"Boring" Isn't Enough.

I completely understand that some of your classes and teachers are very boring. The unfortunate reality is that regardless of how boring your class is, you are still there.

How about we move past saying "it's boring" and find ways to make it more exciting. In my less-exciting classes, I tried . . .

- talking more in class to keep me awake,
- writing notes,
- relating the class to my sport or life, and
- going to the teachers' offices to learn more about them.

These are just some of the tactics you can use, but be creative *and be respectful.*

Play Games against Yourself in School to Create a Competitive Atmosphere.

If you made an 83 on your last test, set a goal to make an 87 on the next one. That way, you are constantly pushing yourself to greatness. You are an athlete. You thrive on competitiveness. So create competitive environments for yourself in the classroom.

WHAT IS DONE IN THE DARK WILL COME TO THE LIGHT

When I committed and signed my letter of intent, my college was swift in sending me a workout plan so I wouldn't be too far behind the other players. The workouts were in a thick booklet that had spring (since I signed in February) and summer workouts.

As I flipped through the booklet, I was amazed first at how long the workouts were. There were fifteen different exercises *just for lifting weights*. Second, I noticed that I didn't know half of the exercises. That's not a knock on my high school strength coach, because he was tremendous, but there was only so much he could show us in our limited time.

After reviewing the booklet, I began working out. I instantly knew that college strength training programs were on a different level from high school. I remember feeling weak and barely being able to finish my workouts in the weight room—not to mention the running, which was much longer and more intense than any running workout I had previously experienced. It felt like my coaches wanted to combine Olympic powerlifting, track, and cross country.

It was tough!

I started consistently completing my workouts around March; I had until my official report date of July 1 to make as much progress as possible.

When I finally started workouts with the team, I was pleasantly surprised. I was in better shape than most of the other freshmen. I realized that those four to five months of work that I had put in individually—especially those times when I did not make my times and had felt embarrassed and weak—really came in handy in front of the whole group. I often finished toward the front in the group runs and handled myself well in the weight room.

It made me realize that as an athlete, what you do in secret individually will be exposed publicly when the team is together.

Think about how you practice in your sport. You typically practice with very little to no fans. The purpose of practice is to make it as game-like as possible with minimal mistakes, but if you happen to make a mistake, the consequences aren't nearly as severe as if you were to do it in a game—as long as you are ready as a team come game day.

Treat your workouts before going to college the same way. If you make every effort to prepare yourself physically before heading to college and joining the team, then you will be ahead of your peers.

SHOW UP PREPARED

As I am sure you have heard your whole life, first impressions are major. When you travel to school and begin your workouts, the last thing you want to do is show up out of shape. When you show up out of shape, you stick out negatively. Coaches will have their eyes on all of your workouts. Instead of sticking out negatively, make sure you are in the best shape possible so coaches are impressed. Here's how you can accomplish this.

1. If your university sends a workout plan, make sure you understand how to properly complete each workout.
2. Assign someone to be your accountability partner to make

sure you are completing the workouts. If you are only completing them by yourself, then it will be easier to skip workouts.

3. Do personal workouts outside of what is given to you. Most workout plans only have weights and conditioning. Take it upon yourself to do personal skills work.

WHEN PRIDE COMES, THEN COMES DISGRACE, BUT WITH HUMILITY COMES WISDOM

The anticipation leading into freshman year is possibly the most nerve-racking time of a young person's life. You are journeying into the unknown. You're excited, because you're experiencing a new level of freedom and maturity, but you're also scared because you're starting off as a small fish in a big pond. For student athletes, this anxiety is intensified because you are finding out whether years of hard work have prepared you for this. You're not sure if you are big enough, fast enough, strong enough, or simply good enough to play collegiate sports.

I remember making my transition to high school football from eighth grade. I was so naïve and didn't have any real expectations. I never thought about playing varsity as a freshman; it was the furthest thing from my mind. I just wanted to be a good athlete and play sports with my friends. Little did I know that three days into fall practice, I would be asked to move up and play varsity.

The transition didn't make me nervous because I didn't know the implications it would have on me as a person and as a football player. I didn't know I would have to show up early to school and watch film; I didn't know how complicated defensive schemes were in high school; I didn't know that linemen on varsity were over 6'5" and 300 pounds. I had no clue, and there I was, thrown onto the field with seventeen/eighteen-year-old men as a fourteen-year-old kid.

There was also a culture shock on the field. The locker room had many conversations that were more advanced than those in my eighth-grade locker room. I didn't party at all, so I was a misfit, to say the least. I simply didn't know how to transition both on and off the field.

Thankfully, there was a person who played my position by the name of Cody Monnette who made it his mission to support me during my transition. He was not the best athlete on the team, but he knew every part of the defensive playbook and was always in the right position. I also had a teammate by the name of Ishmael Harrison who was a phenomenal athlete, and he mentored, taught, and pushed me to be the best athlete possible. Those two really made my transition to high school easier.

Quick side note: If you are currently struggling on or off your playing surface in high school, regardless of your age or grade, I would encourage you to find a mentor who is willing to assist you and has great character. (Refer to the mentor chapter later in the book.)

When I arrived in college, I was feeling the same anxieties as I did with my transition to high school. I was still very naïve, but I understood the magnitude of playing collegiate sports. I felt pressure to be great from my family, teammates, and community—everyone expected me to do great things while I was off at school. Just like high school, there was a different level of ability, film study, and academic rigor in this new setting. Thankfully, another "Cody Monnette" came into my life, and his name was Ryan Walker.

Ryan Walker was a fifth-year senior who was not the best athlete, but he was the smartest player in the room, and he took the time to teach people our very complex playbook. I also had multiple Ishmael Harrisons in teammates Derrick Thompson, Kennan Holman, and Darius Joseph. All of these guys were absolute monsters and hold several records! Although they were the stars of the team, they led with humility and with hard ethics.

Have you played against a team that talked trash constantly, and you couldn't wait to beat them, just to humble them? Or have you ever had a student athlete transfer to your school, and they came maybe from a bigger school than yours, and they were extremely cocky? All you wanted was a shot at them.

This reminds me of a great Bible verse:

> "When someone invites you to a wedding feast, do not take the place of honor, for a person more distinguished than you may have been invited. If so, the host who invited both of you will come and say to you, 'Give this person your seat.' Then, **humiliated**, you will have to take **the least important place**. But when you are invited, take the lowest place, so that when your host comes, he will say to you, 'Friend, move up to a better place.' Then you will be honored in the presence of all the other guests. For all those who exalt themselves will be humbled, and those who humble themselves will be exalted."
>
> — LUKE 14:8–11

When you enter a new situation, it is much better to have a humble attitude with quietness and calmness than pride and loudness. Don't be the cocky freshman. Let coaches and other players see you work hard and compliment, elevate, and brag on others—don't do it yourself. Take a look at the tips that can help you be humble yet powerful.

WHAT MINDSET SHOULD YOU HAVE TRANSITIONING INTO YOUR UNIVERSITY?

The reason I tell you that story is to help you understand that in order for me to have had successful transitions, I needed to be humble enough to allow other people to assist me. As a competitor, I was going back and forth on how to approach these situations.

Similar to most athletes, my first priority was to prove myself as an important piece to the team and show that I was a leader. I wanted to learn the plays before everyone, lead every single drill, and destroy every player that was in front of me. Initially, I had thought that I could handle all of these things by myself, but I quickly realized that I could only go so far without other people. Also, those athletes were upperclassmen, so they knew the campus and how to operate with coaches and teachers: all things that I would have had to figure out myself over a year. These players had warned me of the potential potholes in college athletics to help me transition quicker.

The hardest part about the transition to college is that you had built trust and a reputation at your high school, but in college you have to start over. Your teammates knew you worked hard, they knew your tendencies, and they knew your character. You start thinking, "How can I make a difference? Can I be a vocal leader? If I talk too much, they may think I am annoying. Should I just be quiet and stay in the back?" There were so many questions I had going into college, and looking back, here are some of the things I think can help you with your own transition.

Do Not Go into Your New Situation Cocky and Thinking That You Are Something.

Regardless of your talent level or ranking, there are athletes who more than likely had similar rankings to yours that now also have collegiate experience. The best thing you can do is have confidence in your abilities but observe and ask questions. The upperclassmen know the system, so they can help you. Find great mentors that work their tails off regardless of talent and scholarship. Chances are, there's one guy who does everything the right way, is always in the right place at the right time, and knows the playbook inside and out but is limited in natural abilities. *Attach yourself to this player quickly.*

Don't Forget to Compete!

You can have a mentor and still want to win. Research Kobe Bryant and Michael Jordan. In every way, Kobe wanted to be like Mike and looked to him as a brother. But every time they met on the basketball court, he tried to destroy Mike!

Find Role-Model Players.

Find players on the team with a great work ethic, who are very intelligent, and who have great character; do not necessarily follow the best player on the team. In a perfect world, the best player on the team would have all the previously mentioned attributes, but sometimes they are lazy and arrogant. Think about it this way: find players you can see being coaches one day or act like a coach now. I'm not talking about those players who "think" they know your sport but don't. I'm talking about those players who are another coach on the field with their demeanor and knowledge.

MEDITATE, DON'T MEDICATE

The majority of sports have doctors and athletic trainers for a reason. Doctors and trainers diagnose, evaluate, and treat injuries. The most common practice to heal a sports injury is physical rehab. Doctors and trainers may give you some sort of medication or pill, but they only give it to you for temporary release. The one thing they don't want for you is to become dependent on the medication. If they are good, they should provide a guide for you on how to get back to full strength and self-sufficiency.

I am by no means an expert on mental health, nor am I qualified to give you concrete ways to deal with mental health, but I can offer my humble opinion and advice to assist you in your journey.

FIND A POSITIVE WAY TO RELIEVE STRESS
THAT DOES NOT HARM THE BODY

In a world that is plagued with mental illness caused by stress, anxiety, and various other pressures, it is very important for you to create ways to relieve these pressures without harming yourself both short-term and long-term. There are many bad options available like drugs, alcohol, and even suppressing your emotions, but over time, using these options can lead to detrimental physical and mental effects later in life. Instead, try using one of these alternatives to treat your mental health.

Meditation

Meditation is a great option. Meditation is when you are alone and quiet in a particular place with no music, no TV, and no people. Typically, you lay down with your eyes closed and recite a specific positive phrase (like "I am enough" or "I will be peaceful") that you concentrate on for a certain amount of time. This is done in yoga practices and helps with easing the mind.

In the beginning, it will be hard because your mind will easily travel to your homework, video games, and your last game, but as you practice this more, you will find that you are able to focus your thoughts and finish meditation relaxed.

Prayer

Prayer is another great option. Prayer is different than mediation because you are actively communicating with and showing that you have faith in God. Prayer is a really powerful tool, especially when you have the faith to truly believe that the words you're saying are reaching God and that they have a potential to make a difference. Prayer is not hard. It is the practice of genuinely pouring out your heart and feelings to God and having an expectation that God loves you and wants what is best for you.

All it takes is belief and honesty.

Exercise

Always a great stress reliever.

Therapy

There is nothing wrong with seeing a trained therapist to help you with some of the issues going on in your life. In fact, I encourage you to see a therapist because they are trained and have thousands of hours of experience helping people. There is also nothing wrong with speaking to your family members or loved ones about the situation, if you are comfortable with them. But sometimes they can have the best intentions to help you but end up hurting more than helping.

TAKE ADVANTAGE OF COLLEGE; DON'T LET COLLEGE TAKE ADVANTAGE OF YOU

College coaches are going to work you very hard. They want to put the best product on the field to make them and the university look good. You will constantly be tired, and they will claim a vast majority of your time. At times, you could feel enslaved to them. All those things may be true, but there is a blessing you have: you can work the university just as hard as they are working you by getting a degree, taking advantage of free certifications, joining programs, and talking to alumni.

How? I'm glad you asked. Let's think about college differently.

WHAT SKILL CAN YOU LEARN TO CREATE A BUSINESS, NOT WORK FOR ONE?

You have always been told to "go to school, get a good education, and get a good job so that you have a comfortable life." That's a great thought process, because there is security and good benefits associated with having a job. But what if I told you that there is a community of people who have learned that the knowledge they received in college helps them create a personal business?

I was listening to an interview, and the interviewee said something that was very profound. He said that school gives you a structure, and if you complete certain steps, then you will receive a reward from it. As an example, if you enroll in college and go to class and do your work, at the end you will receive a degree that will allow you to do your certain profession. College is the best, most common way to receive the information you need to obtain a job, which is why people continue to attend. Very few people choose to receive that information and create jobs for themselves.

Similar to being an athlete, it takes long, unusual hours to successfully launch a new business and create enough revenue to sustain the business. Most established organizations you want to work for have founders who created them. They are the ones making the decisions and the money that ultimately control your livelihood. Furthermore, most entrepreneurs start their businesses while they have another full-time job that pays the necessary bills before slowly transitioning to their own business once they make enough money to quit the other job.

The question now is this: How do you use your education to start a business?

Your Main Job Can Be Whichever Degree Path You Choose.

Outside of your primary degree, there is typically space in your schedule to add another major or minor. For example, a student would have a primary degree in education but another major or minor in civil rights. The education degree helps them be a teacher to pay bills, but their passion is civil rights. Utilize your minor, certifications, and other classes to learn a different skillset that can generate more income.

Get Work Experience.

You are going to be tired after school and sport practices, but find time to get real-world experience. Receiving the information is fine, but great leaders understand how to use the information and actually implement the information in a work setting. It is important to learn how to use your knowledge when things are not going perfectly.

Use the Alumni Base.

Alumni are people who have graduated from the school you are wanting to attend. As a student athlete, there are previous student athletes who are successfully leading businesses and have jobs available. The great thing about being an alumni is that you are part of a family of former athletes that played at this particular school. Family takes care of each other, so if you can build relationships with the alumni base, you'll be set.

Use Campus Office Resources.

Use the computers, printers, paper, and other resources at the university to help you in your journey. You do not want to personally pay for these items, so use the school's resources. (Of course, don't steal anything.)

Build Other Relationships on Campus.

Building meaningful and purposeful relationships allows you to evolve and become more well-rounded as a person. Chances are your college years will be the time when you experience the greatest diversity of races, ideas, thoughts, cultures, and languages that you'll ever experience in your life, so take full advantage of it.

Obviously, I had my teammates with whom I spent the majority of my time because of athletic obligations. Then I had a group of friends that would seemingly rotate every semester, because I would build a relationship with a particular person in a class we had together, but when the semester was over, the relationship would fade away. I had my then-girlfriend, now-wife as a friend. I had another group of friends that I played basketball with, and that was the only common ground we had. Then I had some friendships with various staff members across campus. Finally, I had my friends who I shared the same Christian faith with, and we would go on church retreats and have weekly meetings.

I am referencing these relationships because it is important to remember that while you are on campus and a large portion of your time is being given to your sport, you have more interests than just your sport. In hindsight, I noticed that these different friend groups were avenues down which I could explore other dimensions of my life instead of being pigeonholed by sports. I was able to feed my desire for romance, dive deeper into my spiritual life, learn more information professionally, engage socially, and participate in a past-time I loved.

TIMELINE TO ENTREPRENEURSHIP

The following is a loose timeline to assist you in your journey to entrepreneurship. In high school and college, you should focus primarily on the first two steps.

1. Have an idea. (What can you provide to the world?)
2. Write the idea down. (Who is the target audience? Who will it help? Who will pay for it?)
3. Bring the idea to the world. (Market and ask a lot of questions of people who are doing similar things.)
4. Fail and revise the idea. (Adapt, take all feedback, and decide what is important while ignoring people who try to deter you from pursuing the dream.)
5. Expand the idea. (Experience success and talk to more people.)

BUILDING A SOLID MONEY FOUNDATION

I have a very good friend that I respect and hold in high regard. This friend is quite a few years older than me, but we have been friends for well over ten years now. He was actually my junior high coach before he was my friend. In junior high, college was the furthest thing from my mind, but we would often have conversations about his college experience.

He told me that he had had several jobs that made him good money, especially for being a college student. He would always explain these jobs to me in terms of how easy they were and how much fun he had in college doing them. Just like clockwork, he would tell me all those things, then look at me and say, "I have no idea where all that money went." He would tell me how he blew through the money instead of using it to propel his life financially. After years of hearing these stories, I made a vow to myself that I wouldn't go down the same path.

Fast forward to my freshman year of college, and I was finally there. I was in college and had a chance to fulfill my vow of great money management. Unfortunately, I didn't have any money my first two years because I had to live on campus, and they paid for all my expenses.

When I finally starting making money as a junior, it had been so long since I had had money that when I went to my local bank to start a checking account, they said I already had one. I had no idea, because I didn't have money!

Moving on, as a junior I received around $1,500 a month from a stipend check and thought I was ballin'. I only remember having this much money in my possession one other time in my life. Additionally, I had received a Pell Grant check around the same time. I remember getting happy every time I thought about how I would continue to receive this money every month for two more years!

I received my first check at the end of August. I did one good thing by starting a savings account and putting a minimal amount of money away, but that's where my savings for the future ended. I am not typically a big spender, but at the time I had been dating my now-wife for two years. In the beginning, while I was on campus, I could only afford to give her very small gifts for her birthday or other big occasions. I bring that up to say that on her birthday in September, I proceeded to *ball out of control* (according to my standards)! I went to the mall on three separate occasions and ended up spending over $700 on clothes alone.

This spending bug lasted a few more months, and then the Lord revealed to me one day that I was heading down a similar road that I had vowed I would not travel. Thank the Lord that this revelation came, because what I didn't know was that one year later, my car would break down and I would pay $1,500 to get another one. I would continue to fall madly in love with my wife, and I'd need money to buy a ring (I'll keep you all guessing on the price of that) and help pay for a wedding within the next year and a half—and still have money left over to help jump-start my family.

Yes, these were all personal choices that I didn't have to make, but I am thankful that I took my finances seriously so that I could experience these things. By the grace of God, I have the same car that's completely paid for and am still married to my wife.

Don't mess up your future blessings by being bad with money now.

Be Efficient with the "Ball."

In most sports, having the ball is the most important aspect of the game. If you can be efficient while you have the ball, then your chances of winning are much higher. Money management is very similar. The more efficient—or the better you manage—money while you have it, the better. Hear me: I am not saying that you should hold on to every dollar, but you should have a plan.

Most people are scared of, hate, or are bad with money. This is unfortunate, because then people think that money is the source of their problems (which isn't necessarily true). But I do somewhat agree with the saying: "Money is not the answer to everything, but it sure does make things easier." I would add one thing: "Money is not the answer to everything, but *proper money management* sure does make things easier."

This chapter is here to help you build money discipline that, if followed, could help you become a millionaire—legitimately.

LEARN HOW TO MANAGE YOUR MONEY

It doesn't matter whether you are a player on a full-ride scholarship or if you pay every dime of your college tuition as a walk-on. You must still do these three things:

1. Learn how to avoid ruining your future with bad money decisions.
2. Learn how to properly manage money.
3. Learn how to maximize every penny you make, regardless of your income.

This chapter is going to be broken down into two sections. One section will be directed to those athletes on full-ride scholarships, and the second is for those who are either on partial or no scholarship.

SCHOLARSHIP ATHLETES

Scholarship athletes will continue to make more and more money as time progresses. This is a very exciting time for most scholarship athletes. This is the first time they've had complete control over their financial situations, and now they're receiving anywhere from $500 to $2,000 a month in the form of a stipend check. Not only is there a stipend check, but now bigger D-1 universities have what is called a Cost of Attendance check, which can range anywhere from $2,000 to $10,000. Cost of Attendance checks are divided up into four installments throughout the year. Additionally, some student athletes are still eligible for federal financial aid, which could be an additional $5,000 a year. So now what is a student athlete supposed to do with $30,000–$40,000 a year in their pocket?

Sadly, some student athletes, like some average adults, are living paycheck to paycheck and, with two weeks left in the month, struggle for food. How does this happen? Some reasons are very understandable, like helping parents with bills back home, while others are due to student athletes simply being poor with handling money.

So the question still remains: How does a student athlete manage their money well? Let's take a look at some things to consider.

Prioritize Bills and Control Your Splurge Purchases.

Do not ruin your financial future by not paying the bills on time. Then, when you receive a stipend check for the first time, remember that there is nothing wrong with splurging a bit—but make sure that you have an end date. Preferably you would get your first check and buy some of the things you have been dreaming of getting for a long time (still pay your rent!), and then the next month you would slow down and begin thinking about the big picture.

You might dream of having a spouse one day and need to save for a wedding or a ring, or you need to have an emergency fund that pays for unexpected car repairs and trips home. You never know when these issues will arise, and having an emergency fund, as Dave Ramsey says, "can turn a disaster into an inconvenience."

Beware of Too Much Debt.

A big debate in the financial world is whether people should have debt or not. Some people advise you to get credit cards, car loans, and other debt while others advise you to run away from debt. Whether you believe that debt is OK or not, do *not* rack up too much debt.

Debt has interest attached to it, which means that over time you are actually paying more for the item than it was originally priced. If you buy a $10,000 car and want to have it paid off in five years (sixty months), you have $10,000 in debt. If the car has a 3 percent interest rate, you will have paid an extra $781 in interest by the time the car is paid off in full. Some people believe the $781 is worth it, while other people say it is not. The choice is yours.

Learn How to Budget Monthly.

A budget keeps track of all your *income* (what money you make) and *expenses* (what money you spend). A budget is your game plan for money. Without a game plan, you are aimlessly attacking the competition with no plan of victory. If you do that with money, then you will be one of the people who does not know how they've spent their money.

Do this exercise: Grab a piece of paper and draw a line down the middle of the page. On the top of the left side, write "INCOME" and on the right side, "EXPENSES." Under income, write any money you receive on a *monthly basis*; this includes allowances, stipends, job money—write it all. Then, add up all your numbers under income (you should have one number). Under expenses, write every expense you have: rent, car note, Netflix—write it all. Then add up all your numbers under expenses (you should have one number). After you've added up both sides, take your number from income and subtract it from the expenses number.

What did you get? If the number is negative, that means you spend too much. If it's zero, you have exactly the amount you need per month. If it's positive, which is where you want to be, then you can start saving that money.

Build an Emergency Fund.

As mentioned earlier, you should build an emergency fund. This emergency fund is for those times your car breaks down or you need to get home quickly. This fund is not for when you're low on food. This account is for high-cost situations that you should be prepared for so that you are not stuck and left out to dry.

Think about Saving for Retirement.

I know it seems like a long time away, but the earlier you start saving for retirement, the more money you can gain in interest. By simply saving $200 a month from the age of 20 to 65, you can have over a million dollars for your retirement.

Give a Portion of Your Money to Your Local Church or Charity.

I personally give to my church because I am passionate about God and believe that without God, I wouldn't have money. Also, there is something powerful about giving money that you worked hard for to an organization you're passionate about. There is a quote going around that says: "I have never seen a generous person broke." As you exhibit selflessness, you will find out that blessings tend to come back to you.

Learn How to Make Your Money Work for You.

Hardly do people receive money without working for it. You as an athlete receive a stipend check and scholarship because you "work" for the institution. Individuals with jobs exchange their talent and time for a paycheck as well. However, there are avenues available to you that help you make money outside of your primary "job." The following are small descriptions of powerful tools to build money.

1. **High-Interest Savings Account:** These are accounts that are a very safe place to save your money with the smallest chance (technically zero) of losing your money. High interest is anywhere between 1.5 to over 2 percent. Usually big banks like Chase do not give you this type of return, but online and smaller banks will.

2. **Stocks and Bonds:** Simply put, you take a certain amount of money from your check and invest it into businesses through the stock market or with bonds. Since you chose to invest your money with that business, if they succeed, then they will give you a percentage of money to go along with the money you invest.

3. **Real Estate:** Simply, you buy a property, like a house, and have people pay you to live in the house or use the building and pay you monthly rent.

AGE	BEN INVESTS:		ARTHUR INVESTS:	
19	2,000	2,240	0	0
20	2,000	4,749	0	0
21	2,000	7,558	0	0
22	2,000	10,706	0	0
23	2,000	14,230	0	0
24	2,000	18,178	0	0
25	2,000	22,599	0	0
26	2,000	27,551	0	0
27	0	30,857	2,000	2,240
28	0	34,560	2,000	4,749
29	0	38,708	2,000	7,558
30	0	43,352	2,000	10,706
31	0	48,554	2,000	14,230
32	0	54,381	2,000	18,178
33	0	60,907	2,000	22,599
34	0	68,216	2,000	27,551
35	0	76,802	2,000	33,097
36	0	85,570	2,000	39,309
37	0	95,383	2,000	46,266
38	0	107,339	2,000	54,058
39	0	120,220	2,000	62,785
40	0	134,646	2,000	72,559
41	0	150,804	2,000	83,506
42	0	168,900	2,000	95,767
43	0	189,168	2,000	109,499
44	0	211,869	2,000	124,879
45	0	237,293	2,000	142,104
46	0	265,768	2,000	161,396
47	0	297,660	2,000	183,004
48	0	333,379	2,000	207,204
49	0	373,385	2,000	234,308
50	0	418,191	2,000	264,665
51	0	468,374	2,000	298,665
52	0	524,579	2,000	336,745
53	0	587,528	2,000	379,394
54	0	658,032	2,000	427,161
55	0	736,995	2,000	480,660
56	0	825,435	2,000	540,579
57	0	924,487	2,000	607,688
58	0	1,035,425	2,000	682,851
59	0	1,159,676	2,000	767,033
60	0	1,298,837	2,000	861,317
61	0	1,454,698	2,000	966,915
62	0	1,629,261	2,000	1,085,185
63	0	1,824,773	2,000	1,217,647
64	0	2,043,746	2,000	1,366,005
65	0	**$2,288,996**	2,000	**$1,532,166**

I encourage you to research them yourself. (I learned through YouTube.)

NON-SCHOLARSHIP ATHLETES

To my non-scholarship student athletes, unfortunately you do not have the automatic income from the athletic program that scholarship athletes have, but please don't think that you shouldn't even try to make money or act too relaxed while managing your money. The only difference is that you all have to do is make a decision.

Scholarship athletes only have to focus on academics and athletics, but you have the added dimension of finding income while playing sports and keeping your grades high. If you don't have an athletic scholarship but do have an academic scholarship that covers everything for you, then you can operate similarly to the scholarship athletes above.

For student athletes who don't have enough to cover your expenses, the reality of the situation is that you have to make a decision. It is very difficult—nearly impossible—to be great at sports, do well in academics, and work for money simultaneously. At least one of those things will have to go to the back burner at some point. Here are some thoughts on how to navigate through school as a non-scholarship student athlete.

You Have to Take the Scholarship Money That Is Available to You from Schools.

Student loans are not ideal. You pay thousands of dollars in interest, and most people take decades to pay off their loans. So, take the scholarship money. Do not be afraid to go to your school and ask the financial aid office to find money to give to you. Schools don't want people transferring because they want to keep their retention rate high; that's how they make money.

Often, schools offer big scholarships for the first year to get you to go to their school but then take away money for the other three years. Go to your financial aid office and ask what scholarships they have. Remember to be polite but also stern in your asking. Be transparent and say things like, "Hello, I am a student who truly loves going to this institution, but in order for me to maximize my time here, I am in need of financial aid or scholarships." Be persistent! If you receive a no, keep going back. Almost every school has funds. You just have to make sure you receive them.

Complete the FAFSA and Receive a Pell Grant.

The federal Pell Grant is free money if your family's income level is under $50,000. Filling out the Free Application for Federal Student Aid (FAFSA) is a lengthy process, so just make sure you set time aside and that you have your family's tax information with you.

Typically, FAFSA is available to be filled out on or after October 1 of the year prior to you needing it, and it typically closes June 20 prior to the next semester's start. (Although they almost always extend the deadline, but there is no guarantee funds will be available past the deadline.)

Choose Your Priorities.

I mentioned that you can't be great at three things at one time, but you can possibly rotate priorities. If your sport is in the fall, maybe you focus on your sport and academics while your finances are put on the back burner. Then, in the off-season, you switch.

I know this sounds great in theory, but how do you actually do it?

Pace Your Spending.

If your sport's season is in the fall, then during the summer you work and make money. Then, think toward the future and save some of your money for the following school year. Project and see how much you might spend during the semester and save for it. It will take strong discipline to make sure you are taken care of every year.

Make Your Money Work for You.

It is very important to make your money work for you by making more wealth while you're away from your job. Look into a high-interest savings account (discussed in the last section). You don't have the luxury of working very much, especially during the season, so when you *do* work, a high-interest savings account will make your financial situation easier.

Stick to a Budget.

Make sure that you budget and do not live above your means. Because you are choosing to pursue athletics, you have to strategically plan your money so that you can survive the year with low levels of stress.

Obviously, if you have your funds secure, then follow the directions for a scholarship student athlete.

CORE VALUES

Most sports teams have a set of core values they often say or have hung up in the locker or weight room. Coaches usually say their teams have hard work, discipline, enthusiasm . . . and the list goes on and on. These words are your team's core values. Coaches usually pick these words because they believe successful programs have these elements. When things get tough, the program can revert back to the core values to get them through. This chapter will aim to help you develop your own personal core values.

I was extremely nervous heading into college, especially as an athlete. My perception of college was partying every weekend, girls, and alcohol and drugs. I thought players would constantly try to pressure me into experimenting with various drugs, alcohol, and other activities. I personally didn't want to become one of those athletes that began doing all those things and having it affect my play on the field, classwork, and relationships. I don't know why, but I assumed that one day I would just be forced to do these activities.

(Side note: there is nothing wrong with people who decide to partake in those activities within the law. These were just activities I personally didn't want to be a part of my life.)

My perspective changed about a year and a half prior to starting college. My life was drastically changed because I completely gave my life over to Jesus Christ and became a Christian. I quickly began to take my faith seriously. The relationship I began to have with Jesus gave me a set of core values that would guide the way I lived my daily life.

For example, as I was transforming, I started changing the way I talked. For a fifteen-, sixteen-, and seventeen-year-old, I had a foul mouth. I made a covenant with myself to not drink or smoke because my family has had individuals with drug and alcohol abuse. Also, I wanted to treat people better. I was an arrogant, close-minded, mean athlete that knew when to be nice and when to cause trouble so that the right people knew I was "a good kid." To summarize, my transformation helped me begin to create a set of core values to stand on so that I was not easily influenced by different people.

YOUR CORE VALUES ARE THE ROOT OF WHO YOU ARE

The previous story described how I came to live by my personal set of core values. Don't feel as though your core values have to be the same as my core values or anyone else's. The most important thing is that you have core values, so that when you have to make a tough decision, you have a system to help you.

The hardest part about core values is that sometimes your core values are different from other people's. This means you will have to take a stand sometimes and decide whether you will stand for you values or compromise to make yourself look better in front of your friends.

There is an old saying: "If you do not stand for something, you will fall for anything." This means that if you do not have a set of values that guide and direct your life, then you will more than likely do anything others are telling you to do.

How do you develop these core values?

Find a Role Model to Look Up To.

Think about the belief system of an individual who has shaped your life in a positive manner. For example, I adopted not drinking and smoking from my dad. He saw how drugs and alcohol affected his family, so he decided to not partake. For some people, they have been taught to be extremely loyal and that regardless of the situation, loyalty comes above everything else. For some it might be honesty, others trustworthiness, and others respecting elders. There is not a set number of core values you should have. It's completely up to you.

Use Your Core Values at Every Opportunity.

Every opportunity that comes your way is a chance to demonstrate and use your core values. If these values are not put into practice, then they are not "core values" but rather good ideas. For instance, if your core value is honesty and you are constantly being dishonest, then you are not being true to your core values.

Core Values Take Time to Develop.

The previous tip encourages you to take every opportunity to demonstrate your core values, but if you have a slip-up, especially in the beginning, don't beat yourself up about it. Treat it like your sport: you want to execute every play right, but sometimes you don't. When you don't execute properly, you move on to the next play, and when the game is over, you watch film and correct it. If you don't demonstrate your core values, continue with the rest of your day. Later that night, reflect on it and fix it moving forward.

PART III

BEGINNING COLLEGE

SET A STANDARD

One month into my brother starting college, he called me to talk about some recent struggles he had been having with his teammates. They were asking him to go and party, but he really did not want to participate. He said he noticed that before college, I had established a set of core values and had never wavered from them.

As he continued, I instantly thought back to my first six months of college. Every weekend I was being asked to go to this party or that pregame or other functions. I knew that if I decided to party one time, then all the previous times I said "no" would be a waste because they would continue asking. It took close to six months for people to fully accept that I would never go to any function. Close to two years after holding to this standard, my teammates began telling new student athletes that I would not participate in parties. I realized that by me doing the dirty work early in college, my remaining three and a half years were easy.

For other people, there is nothing wrong with going to these functions so long as all parties are abiding by the law. As I mentioned in the previous chapter, I did not have a desire to attend these events. I ended up telling my brother exactly what I had told myself: you have to set a standard for who you are. Some of my teammates were embraced earlier than I was because they looked forward to going to parties and had a great time out on the town. They set a standard for themselves just like me. The standard I set just wasn't as popular within the team as theirs.

When I think about setting a standard, I think about when I was an athlete and would play "those" teams, the ones that seemed like they just never made mistakes. The crazy thing was that these teams weren't very talented, but they played very smart and weren't going to beat themselves. It is impossible for me to know, but I bet one of the core values on those teams was discipline.

I can imagine drills at every practice focused on limiting mental errors and not beating themselves. I can see the coach constantly saying, "We aren't good enough to win off talent, so we have to be disciplined." Eventually over time, the team would make the core values a way of life, but it started with a standard being created. This chapter will help you set a standard in a new environment.

You are transitioning to a new environment, and the core values that you have developed are the values that you are going to set a standard for. Put simply, setting a standard means you're letting everyone know how you are going to act and talk while in this environment. Your actions will establish your identity. You have a blank slate to create your identity at the university.

But sometimes, setting a standard can be tough in the beginning. For some of you, it will be relatively easy for you to set a standard because your values align with most of your teammates'. For others, you may have a little more resistance and find it harder to transition and be accepted in your new environment. Regardless, you shouldn't conform your values to fit in with others. Conforming to others may help you build relationships quicker, but in the long run you will feel incomplete because you are not being your true self. As a result, you must establish a standard that you will live out your core values. So how do we set a standard?

You Must Be Consistent with Your Core Values.

After you have established your core values internally, you must actively show your values externally to your new team and environment. You show your values by saying you are loyal and not talking behind your friend's back. If you value positivity, you stay positive whether you're playing in games or not.

In the long-term, people value consistency over flashiness. If you cave in one time and fall victim to the peer pressure, then you are essentially starting over. You are not supposed to be perfect, but you communicate your values during those times when you might not be able to uphold a commitment.

Push through Hard Times.

If you are a student athlete who has discovered that your core values are different than those of most people you encounter, then it is important that you push through the difficult and lonely times.

It Is Perfectly Fine to Create a New Standard for Self.

College is where people evolve and change because they are learning how to become independent adults. It is normal for people to start one way as a freshman and then as a junior or senior decide they want to do things differently. Personally, you shouldn't feel bad, weird, or awkward for wanting to make this change. The only people who will give you backlash are people who you are becoming different from.

You might have friends you have been cool with for years, but now you want to change and they're not ready yet. That is OK. Just understand that when you want to make a change, people will treat you as if you aren't serious or are joking for a while. This might make it a little tougher for you because you are having to tear down the other reality of who you are, lay a foundation for the new you, and build on top of that—and unfortunately, the hardest part is tearing down your old identity.

COMMUNICATION IS KEY!

I'm going to give you two personal accounts of my communication. One instance was terrible, and the other was a good example. Let's start with the terrible.

It was midway through my sophomore year at SMU and I was playing average football. Good enough to start a few games, but I also didn't play much in the other games. Halfway through practice, as we prepared for our seventh game, I found out my grandfather had passed away. The funeral would be on a Friday, the day before a game.

I told my head coach the situation, but I didn't tell my position coach, intentionally, what was going on. We didn't have the best relationship, and out of stubbornness I thought that by me not telling him, I would somehow get over on my coach.

Every Friday, we had a meeting before going to the hotel, and during the meeting my position coach asked where I was and my teammates told him. The next day while I was warming up, he approached me. I can't remember his exact words, but he was very irritated that I had not told him. As a result, not only did I sit on the sideline all that game, but I didn't play in the next two games either.

Obviously I didn't get benched because my grandfather passed away but because I didn't tell him where I was, which was irresponsible. I thought that by not telling him, I would avoid a tough conversation and get over on my coach. But in the end, I was only hurting myself.

The second story is less dramatic. (For some reason, the good parts of stories are usually less dramatic.) In my senior year, I was heading to a film and practice session after a game when my car stopped working completely. It wouldn't even move. As soon as this happened, I pulled out my phone and called my strength and conditioning coach and all the appropriate people to make sure they knew where I was. In the end, it took six hours to take care of everything, but my coaches were much more understanding this time around because I effectively communicated. There was no punishment, and I didn't hear anything else about it.

It's imperative that you learn how to effectively communicate as a student athlete. These tips for effective communication apply to you as a student athlete but also will play a major role in your post-college life. I didn't realize how much college athletes communicate at practice and during competition (in most sports). It seemed like every second I was sending a nonverbal or verbal signal!

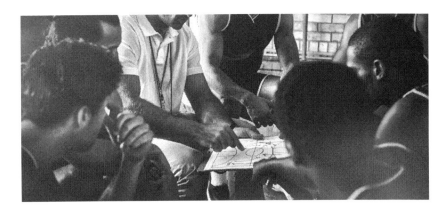

As a student, I was shocked by the amount of emails I received. Emails are the primary way professors send information and the primary way I could contact them when I had questions.

Often, we don't do things because we don't understand why we need to do them. Effective communication is one of those phrases that people say but don't explain why it's important. The "why" behind effective communication is as follows:

1. It eliminates confusion. It's nearly impossible to know the mind of another individual, so when we effectively communicate, we clearly explain our thoughts and actions to another individual. For instance, if you give up a big play to the opposition and you think it's your teammate's fault, but they think it's your fault, then you can talk to each other and get each other's perspective to prevent it from happening again.

2. Not only does effective communication eliminate confusion, but it allows a person to control the narrative. For example, if you miss practice without communicating and don't tell your coaches why, then you are allowing the coach to assume you don't care. But if you take control and explain why, then your coach will understand your situation. We never want people to guess; we want to tell them.

3. We would rather be proactive rather than reactive. There are so many situations that could've been handled better if people had communicated before it became a big issue.

Understand When to Communicate.

The obvious answer would be to always communicate no matter the circumstance. While that is true, there are certain circumstances where you must communicate quickly and accurately.

1. Anytime you are running late for class, practice, or any other engagement. You need communicate as soon as you realize you will be late.

2. When you are confused about an assignment in class or

practice. It is better for you to completely understand what is expected of you than to let the embarrassment of asking a question lead to you making a mistake.

3. Anytime you want to learn more about a topic.

Know the Channels of Communication.

Knowing how to communicate or in what way you should communicate is extremely important as well. Your options include:

1. Face-to-face. Any time there is a major conflict, or you need an extended time to talk, or if it's a personal matter, then talk face-to-face. Face-to-face allows you to talk in private because there is no paper trail associated like with texting or email. Face-to-face is better because you can read the other person's body language and hear the tone in which they are saying something. You won't have to guess.

2. Phone conversations are for those instances where you want to hear their tone, but you are long distance or can't possibly meet in person.

3. Email is the most professional way to communicate (outside of in-person meetings). This is most prevalent in schools and businesses because you sometimes want to have a conversation thread of written communication for liability.

4. Texting is becoming more popular, but this should be your last option for communication.

WHAT AM I GETTING MYSELF INTO?

As you progress to more advanced stages in life, there will be more responsibilities associated with be ing a student athlete. When I was in elementary school, academics was the most important aspect of my life. We learned fundamentals like addition and subtraction, and there were no organized sports at my school. I still played on sports teams, but we only had two two-hour practices a week.

When I moved up to junior high school, the pressure of academics intensified. Not only was my athletic participation determined by my ability to pass classes, but also in eighth grade, I began taking a high school algebra class, which, as we discussed, had a major impact on my future. Athletically, we had two-hour practices every weekday we didn't have games. At the same time, we began incorporating various strength and conditioning methods to help us with our athleticism.

Then in high school, I started hearing about class rank, passing standardized testing, enrolling in college, and many other pressures that intensified my academics. Athletically, we began traveling more for games; the level of intensity in practice and weight training increased significantly; we incorporated small amounts of film study.

Now all of these were in place to help me gain a collegiate scholarship.

My goal was to attend college on a scholarship, but I realized that collegiate athletics was far different than any other experience. Practices were listed as two hours each, but really, they were three and a half hours. You had to get out there early for stretching and your personal warm-up. Then you had a pre-practice walk-through before warm-up with the team. And then practice would start, and after it was over you had post-practice responsibilities. We were expected to lift weights at least three times a week. Plus we had meetings and film study, and then we'd travel for games, usually to a different state, which would last for hours.

When people tell you about collegiate sports, they are quick to tell you the good stuff: games, gear, and notoriety. But you hardly hear about the number of hours it takes. Maybe if you knew about the schedule beforehand, you might choose to not play and focus your attention elsewhere. Kobe Bryant said that if he knew beforehand what it took to be as great of a basketball player as he was, then he wouldn't have done it.

This chapter is simply to give you a breakdown of your anticipated schedules in college. It is important to note that different universities and sports have different schedules. This is just to give you a glimpse into what life could be like.

IN-SEASON SCHEDULE

The in-season schedule is the busiest you'll be throughout the year. The NCAA has rules saying that you are allowed to participate in twenty hours a week of sport-related activities. But as a collegiate student athlete, you can easily spend over fifty hours a week or more on your sport—that is *before* academics, eating, your social life, or internships.

How so? Let's break down your weekly schedule.

Actual Practice: 6–17.5 Hours

Obviously, you have regularly scheduled practices four to five times a week that range between an hour and a half to three and a half hours. You have a personal warm-up, the warm-up with your position group, a team pre-practice walk-through, a team warm-up, practice, and post-practice drills.

Team Meetings: 5–10 Hours

You have film sessions or meetings with your coaches and teammates. Most of the time, there are meetings every single day that range from one to two hours. Then there are team meetings with the head coach, position meetings, and NCAA compliance meetings that go over the NCAA amateur rules.

Weight and Conditioning: 3–6 Hours

These mandatory weight and conditioning trainings occur three or four times a week and last from an hour to an hour and a half.

Travel: 6–12 Hours

You have to travel to the location of your competitions. Colleges are not like high schools where you drive one hour the day of the game. You are more than likely leaving your state, which means long bus rides or plane flights the day before. The process of leaving your school and arriving at your destination takes between six and twelve hours. Additionally, the whole day of the game is geared toward getting ready for competition, which obviously is all day.

School Classes: 12–15 Hours Plus Studying

Academically, you are required to take at least twelve hours a semester, and most advisors push you to take fifteen hours so that if you drop a class, you are still eligible to play. Those twelve to fifteen hours are solely class time; you also spend one to three hours a day studying, writing, or doing something related to schoolwork—per class.

Personal Life: Various

Then you need to find time for all other personal activities: organizations, building friendships, eating, networking, and connecting with family.

OFF-SEASON

Most sports have a period of time when they are in-season and a period of time when they are not in-season (the off-season). In the off-season, the NCAA rule is that you can only have eight hours dedicated to sport-related activities. If your sport has an off-season period where you can train similar to in-season (i.e., spring football practice), then it goes back to the twenty hours a week for a given time.

Similar to in-season, the off-season schedule is manipulated to fit within the legal number of hours. There are several "voluntary workouts and meetings" that the whole team shows up to, but for the most part you are hovering around fifteen to twenty hours, so you have more flexibility within your schedule. Make sure that you maximize this time to focus on academics or internships and build relationships on campus.

Weight and Conditioning: 10–12.5 Hours

Mandatory weight training and conditioning sessions are the priority and happen five times a week. The weight lifting portion can last an hour or two. The conditioning portion is usually an hour or an hour and a half.

"Voluntary" Workouts: 2–3 Hours

These are usually player-led workouts that last an hour two or three times a week.

Team Meetings: 1–2 Hours

Periodic team meetings and films might happen for an hour once or twice a week.

School Classes: 12–15 Hours Plus Studying

Just like for your in-season semester, you are required to take at least twelve hours a semester, and most advisors push you to take fifteen hours so that if you drop a class, you are still eligible to play. Those twelve to fifteen hours are solely class time. You also spend one to three hours a day studying, writing, or doing something related to schoolwork.

Personal Life: Various

Then you still need to find time for all other personal activities: organizations, building friendships, eating, networking, and connecting with family.

SUMMER SCHEDULES

Not all athletes are required to stay on campus. If you are a scholarship athlete, you might be expected to attend summer school. Outside of your freshman year, the summer is the most freedom you will have while in college. You still have workouts, but usually you only have one or two classes. (Plus, classes are usually easier in the summer.) The majority of your day is still available. During this time, you can either waste it or use it to set yourself up for your future!

Weight and Conditioning: 10–12.5 Hours

Mandatory weight training and conditioning sessions are the priority and happen five times a week. The weight lifting portion can last an hour or two. The conditioning portion is usually an hour or an hour and a half.

"Voluntary" Workouts: 2–3 Hours

These are usually player-led workouts that last an hour two or three times a week.

Team Meetings: 1 Hour

There are team meetings, but they do not happen often. Schedule one hour a week.

School Classes: 3–6 Hours Plus Studying

Academically, you may have one or two classes that take up three to six hours a week in class. Of course, you'll have a couple of hours to complete assignments. Classes are usually easier because you have a shorter amount of time and professors do not have time to grade all the papers thoroughly.

All Other Personal Activities: Various

This is the time where you make sure you visit your family members and invest in relationship building, Also, this is the time where you set up internship opportunities, informational interviews, or summer jobs. The summer is when you explore your opportunities outside of sports. Whether you have a one-year collegiate career or a twenty-year professional career, you will need another career when you finish playing. The sooner you explore your options, the easier the transition will be.

SCHEDULING WINS CHAMPIONSHIPS

I went to school probably thirty minutes away from where my parents lived. Regardless of the distance, I severely missed home and traveled home every single weekend. (My friends in school constantly made fun of me for this.) Every Friday, I would heavily anticipate going home. In the off-season, our football coaches made it a point to have our workouts finish in the morning so we could enjoy our weekend. The biggest scheduling mistake I ever made was having two Friday classes: one at 9 a.m. and the other at 1 p.m. That random 1 p.m. class would continually prolong my time getting home by at least five hours.

In most sports, there is a regular season and then playoffs. In these sports, the regular season determines your post-season ranking. Simply put, the more wins you have in the regular season, the higher your seeding for the playoffs. This comes with less travel, easier teams, and more home games. The interesting aspect about the regular season schedule is that it isn't the same for every team. There are many factors, such as quality of competition, amount of away games, stretches where you play tough competition back-to-back-to-back, and many more.

These factors may be the difference between the #1 seed and #3 seed in the playoffs, which significantly decreases your chances of winning a championship. In this chapter, I will give you a few things to consider while scheduling for your semester in college.

In college, there aren't any six- or nine-week breaks. Everything is broken down by the semester, or four-month increments (summer school is a little different). But there are some tips that can help you as an athlete. This does not take the place of your academic advisor. Rather, these are tips for you to keep in mind to help you get rest and study for you to be effective.

Friday Classes Are the Worst!

No matter your degree program or sport, try your best to avoid Friday classes. You might want to go home after workouts to chill, and not having these classes can get you home earlier. If you cannot avoid these classes, then take the earliest classes you can.

Eat Lunch.

Do not forget to schedule time to sit down for lunch or time to grab a lunch on the way to class (if your professor or coach lets you eat in class).

Avoid Time Breaks.

Try not to have awkward breaks in your schedule unless it is to eat or study. Large unused blocks can get irritating because you don't have quite enough time to nap—and you might want to.

Utilize Your Summers.

After freshman year, your summer schedules will be the easiest to handle, so take advantage and get some experience that will help you in your career field. During the year, you won't have as much time, and you will be tired. So when you have free time, be productive.

THE FRESHMAN WALL!

I reported to my university in July, which was enough time to take two summer school classes, start workouts with the team, and do football camp before the season started. In July, I was doing very well in my classes and felt I was doing well in the workouts. (I had also started a new relationship with a fine young lady.)

Then came August and fall camp, which was fourteen hours of football a day. It stretched me tremendously! I started camp off very strong, but around the second of the three weeks of practice, my performance dropped tremendously. My first week went well, because when you're a freshman, they give you a small workload to see if you can handle it before putting more and more on your plate. Come the second week, my position coach dumped the whole kitchen sink on me to see how I would respond, and it did not go well.

I had a very bad day of practice on a Tuesday, and I got destroyed in the meeting that afternoon. I was not used to getting chewed out like that, and it had an effect on me because I am a people pleaser and like to do well in front of my coach and teammates. This one day led to a downward spiral over the next few weeks where I think I dropped more passes than I caught in practice. At the same time, my girlfriend and I had begun having massive arguments and were on the verge of breaking up multiple times. To add insult to injury, my 4.0 GPA from the summer fell all the way down to a 2.4 during the first semester.

Live shot of me fumbling at Texas A&M

Looking back, I realize I didn't have the mental toughness required, and I didn't know how to overcome issues in my life. Everything came crashing down in what I believe ended up being the biggest game I ever played in.

Still in my freshman year, we were playing an SEC team. At the time, their stadium held close to ninety thousand people, which was a big difference compared to the biggest crowd I'd played in front of in high school, which was probably eight thousand, if I'm being generous. To add on to the pressure, around twenty of my high school classmates went to this particular university.

Despite my struggles, my coaches still allowed me to play and work through my issues. I played tight end, so in this particular game, my job was to help our linemen block the other team's defensive linemen for a moment and not allow them to get to our quarterback, then slowly backpedal and be an option for our quarterback if he needed help.

I went in to do my job on one particular play. I hit one of the other team's linemen, then I started my backpedal. The quarterback threw me the ball, and the rest happened so fast I barely knew what happened. I caught the ball and began to bring it close to my body, but the next thing I knew I got hit and—*BOOM!*—the ball came out of my hand. I realized that not only had I fumbled, but the other team had picked up the ball and scored a touchdown.

To this day, I remember how small I felt in a stadium filled with over ninety thousand people cheering because of my mistake. After all that had transpired over the course of two months, this was devastating to my confidence and ability to thrive away from home. Thankfully, I was eventually able to recover and move on while in college.

Let's take a look at some of the lessons I learned throughout this time and how I ultimately overcame this issue.

You remember that first off-season workout after winter or summer break? You feel so sluggish and out of space, don't you? Think about the time you moved up to high school, and you played more games in-season, and it felt like the season would never end. In both scenarios, you feel great in the beginning because you have adrenaline, and then—*WHAM!*—you feel like you hit a wall. Your body hasn't done this type of training in a year, or this is the first time you've played this many games, and it takes time to adjust.

Your freshman year in college will feel the same way at some point. It is bigger than just sports. Maybe it'll be in academics, family, relationships, home sickness—inevitably you will hit a wall. There is no shame in hitting a wall, but it is important get over the wall as quickly as possible. Here's how.

THE FRESHMAN WALL IS REAL!

In college, you will have to keep up an unprecedented level of energy and focus on a season. It'll be more than you've ever done in your life. For every single practice and game, you have to be prepared, or you will get replaced or embarrassed. I had a teammate tell me that basically as a collegiate athlete, you perfect the art of being productive while you are tired. You are always tired, but you push through.

Not to turn this into a negative situation, but during your first semester or year, there will be some bumpy times along your journey. It is perfectly normal. It will not a big deal if you have some issues with family, since you might be gone for a long time, or if your academic or athletic performance slips a little, or if your social life gets out of whack.

Adjust to Play Time.

The most common hurdle I see for incoming freshmen is that you go from playing every play in high school to either not playing or playing very little in college. It's a big learning curve physically and mentally for most student athletes. Most are truly not ready, but every freshman thinks they are. Regardless of whether you think you are or not:

1. Don't take this time to hang out and party all the time and sacrifice your future. Often, student athletes build bad habits that first year when they don't play, and the habits you create early can follow you. You could be labeled as a bad teammate, lazy, or not focused.
2. Understand that you only need one opportunity to succeed. You need to prepare every day to ready yourself for when your number is called—and when it is called, go dominate.

Keep the Problem Area the Problem Area.

It is normal to feel overwhelmed in school or in sports, so that's not a problem. The problem is when you let one area impact other areas.

Do not let it seep into other areas of your life, because it will feel like your whole life is falling apart at once.

If your problem is on-field issues, then keep it in the athletic facility. If you take it to your relationships, it isn't received well and could mess up the relationship. Find the source of the issue and do everything in your power to overcome it as quickly as possible. Do not be afraid to face your issues and address them quickly.

As a matter of fact, you won't move on until you do.

Find and Destroy Problems.

When you identify the problem, focus your energy on getting that area fixed. If the problem is sports, spend more time working out or talking to your coach. Focus on getting that area fixed, and make sure when you go to sleep that night, you reflect on one victory in that area. We do not want this problem to grow larger until it seems incomprehensible to overcome.

If you need to work on your spiritual life, take time to pray more and fast. If you are feeling severely homesick, then talk to your family members more or talk to a counselor. If you need to take time away from family and friends to attack the problem, make sure that you communicate with those parties so they do not think something is wrong with you or that you're mad at them.

Find Momentum.

After you receive one victory, keep setting new goals so that you keep the momentum. We discussed momentum in the Transition of Power chapter.

This Too Shall Pass.

In the best book in the world, the Bible, there is a whole passage dedicated to time in the book of Ecclesiastes, chapter 3. It starts out by saying, "There is a time for everything." I bring this up because regardless of the struggles you might be having in an area, there is always an end point.

If your problem area is sports and you just can't seem to overcome some things, thankfully there is a final game of the season. At the end of the season, take a brief period of time to reflect and see some of the areas you might need to work on, then celebrate the successes you achieved and quickly put the season as a whole behind you. Hit the restart button.

The same goes with academic life. The semester ends with finals, so regardless of whether you did great or poorly, hit the reset. I think the Lord has given us a great gift in that while we are on earth, we have the opportunity to have new beginnings and start fresh.

* * *

I think a sign of maturity is being able to not only restart at the conclusion of an event but also being able to restart while you are in the midst of something. I heard an interview by an amazing NFL quarterback, Russell Wilson. They were asking Wilson to describe his approach between each play. Wilson said that while he receives the play from a coach, he listens, then right before going into the huddle to talk to his teammates, he closes his eyes and imagines that he is hitting a reset button. He says he does that every single play.

To me, that is the ultimate sign of maturity, for all aspects of life: the ability to release whatever happened seconds prior and focus on the next opportunity you have.

A MENTOR'S HINDSIGHT IS YOUR FORESIGHT

A wise man learns from others' mistakes, not their own.

We've gone on a wild journey throughout this book. This last chapter will be not only the longest but the most in-depth because I am so passionate about mentorship. Mentorship changed my life, and I am so thankful that people took the time to invest in me.

I would be remiss if I didn't mention the first two mentors in my life: my mom and dad. They continually gave me insight and put me in front of people who had insight to help lead and guide me through life, and for that I am forever grateful. I encourage any athlete reading this book who has parents, one parent, grandparents, or aunts and uncles who take the time to be a resource to you to not only thank them but listen to their advice. They have lived longer than you, and they know more than you! I can probably say without fear of contradiction that there have been well over forty people who have served as a mentor for me. I don't want to name names for fear of leaving anyone out, but there is one mentor relationship that I have had beyond my parents that has recently changed the trajectory of my life.

I met my mentor at the most pivotal point of my life to that point. I had just finished my football career at SMU. Prior to this moment, my whole life was about sports, God, and my family. My identity was in being a good collegiate athlete. I had recently made the decision to forgo training for the NFL to explore different options. The only problem was I didn't feel as though I had a true skillset for a job. I hadn't prepared myself as well I could have for the next steps. (Like I'm urging you to do!) As a result, I figured I would teach and coach, just like my dad.

One day, while I was working my part-time job at the university, someone I barely spoke with at the time came to me and asked about my post-graduation plans and if I wanted to get a master's degree. Even though I hadn't taken my bachelor's degree very seriously, the thought of a master's degree was something that had crossed my mind. My mom and dad had both made it a point to tell me that if I ever had the chance to get master's degree, take it. So, I was intrigued.

Over the next few weeks, she and I talked, and it slowly became real. This was an opportunity for a new beginning.

I wanted to invest more in my education, so I began treating the master's application process very seriously. After a series of events, praise God that I received admission into the only program I had applied to. I would be working as a graduate assistant with my mentor, the woman who encouraged me to pursue my master's.

I learned so much from my master's program, but the information I learned from my mentor was by far the best thing that happened. She invested in me and poured over fifteen years of experience into me. She taught me how to be a Christian in the workplace. She allowed me and my wife to come dine with her family. She indirectly gave me more time to explore personal interests that the school provided. She let us watch her dogs. She allowed me to interrupt her during her daunting tasks and hold her hostage with conversations that lasted hours. She sternly corrected me when I would complete a task wrong. And lastly, she loved me for me and taught me how to show grace not only in the workplace, but in life.

Her willingness to mentor me helped me in my marriage, start my first job, write my first book, and discover my purpose in life. To this day, I am forever indebted to her for the sacrifices she continually made for me! Great mentors are hard to find, but when you find one . . . you better keep them.

Think of a mentor like the good leader on a team. During practices and workouts, that team leader is usually in front of the line to demonstrate the proper technique for drills. The leader has been there for a while and knows what it takes to be successful in that particular position. Leading the front of a line is more than just a position: it is a responsibility, because every other person behind you in line is watching your every move to make sure they're doing it right, to please the coach, and become better athletes by using the right technique. If the leader uses the proper technique, every other person can follow those keys to success. But if they do not use proper technique, then the coach must stop the drill to point out the mistake and ask the leader to repeat the drill using the proper technique.

Mentors in life work the same way. They have already gone through leading and using proper techniques, and they have also experienced life correcting them and having to start over.

THE DIFFERENCE BETWEEN SUCCESS AND STAGNANCY

Great mentors are the deciding factor between why some people thrive and why some people have an abundance of talent but never reach their full potential. People think that because they are talented, they will be able to make it in life by themselves. That is far from the truth. Every successful person has a mentor, whether you know it or not.

Mentors are those people that you admire because they have reached a level of greatness or stature in an area of their life that you want to learn how to experience for yourself. Mentors are different from people you "idolize." Idols are those mystical people you might not ever meet, but you pattern some of your behaviors after them, fantasize meeting them, and are a genuine fan of their work.

Mentors, on the other hand, are accessible people who have either determined that you have potential and want to invest their time, resources, and energy to assist you, or they are people you have sought out for help. Regardless, mentors can serve you in various ways. They can write letters of recommendation, walk you through a process step by step, get you in contact with high-level individuals, create opportunities you would have never thought were imaginable, and change the trajectory of your family's life.

However, it is possible to find bad mentors. Here are a few tips to help you find the right one.

Find a Quality Mentor.

How much information do they really have? Have they made an impact? Do they have connections? A mentor has to have extensive wisdom in a particular area. Wisdom and knowledge are better than having a cool title. The ultimate goal is for your mentor to have wisdom, which can come in one of two forms.

1. The highest level of wisdom, which comes from God.
2. Wisdom that is the result of practiced knowledge.

Sometimes, chasing a mentor who has a cool title can be great, but you will gain the most out of mentors who have the ability to make sound decisions in the field and can teach you to do the same, to demonstrate wisdom.

Also, if possible, you want someone who has made a significant impact in the field. If you want to teach, have they discussed an innovative teaching style? If you want to coach, have they created a new system or way of doing things? If you want to be an engineer, have they been a part of a team that built an innovative system overseas? Find someone who has made an impact.

Lastly, consider if this potential mentor has built meaningful relationships that can help you in the future.

How Do You Ask Someone to Be Your Mentor?

Most mentorships happen organically. It may be a teacher that you visit with often or a supervisor you have a natural chemistry with. These relationships are great because you've already established a level of trust with them—all you have to do now is be purposeful in your communication and ask for the help you need.

If you want a mentor that you haven't built a relationship with before, then you should ask that individual if you can take them out for lunch. People love lunch (they have to eat), especially when someone else pays for it. When you reach out to them, make sure that you have meaningful questions to ask. There is nothing worse than sitting at a lunch in silence. It feels like a waste of time. Yes, you gave them a free meal, but neither one of you benefitted from the interaction. From there, you'll probably not continue to communicate. So make sure you have good questions.

Furthermore, when you ask a question, let the other person talk more than you. If you had all the answers, then you would not be at the lunch with this person. Of course, contribute to the conversation casually, but let the other person talk more while you listen and take notes.

Know Where You Are.

Understand that your dream mentor might not be accessible immediately, but there are other people being mentored by that person who may be available. For example, Serena Williams can't mentor you as a high school tennis player, but maybe she has other college tennis players under her tutelage who can mentor you. Do not feel like you are too good for these people. Let them train and mentor you. Their mentorship will help you get to their level, and then when you progress, maybe you can eventually get to where the Serena Williamses of the world want to mentor you. If you blow off the "little people," then the elite will not want to mentor you anyway.

Have Multiple Mentors.

Do not be afraid to have multiple mentors in different areas. There is nothing wrong with having a mentor for your academics, another for your sport, another for your spiritual life, another for your career, and another to help you monetarily. Often, people get in trouble because they have a mentor and think that mentor's word carries as much weight in one field as it does in another. People have specialties, which means they may know a few things in other areas, but they are not the same level of expert in them as they are in their specialty field.

If your field is science and your science teacher has agreed to serve as a mentor for you to help you in science, that's amazing. But if that same science teacher played your particular sport in high school, that does not necessarily mean that you should have them as a mentor in your sport. There is no harm in finding multiple mentors.

They won't get offended, because chances are, they have done the same thing.

Find a Mentor Who Values Truth.

No matter what, you have to find a mentor who does not mind telling you the truth. Often, people have mentors who are significantly older than themselves. For example, Sean Combs, a.k.a. P. Diddy, is fifty years old with a net worth over $800 million. His mentor is a seventy-year-old guy named Ray Dalio, whose net worth is over $18 *billion.* Even though the money difference does help prove my point, what I want you to understand is that older people don't put your feelings over their desire for you to succeed. As long as they tell you the truth, you'll get over it.

The mentors who tell you the truth realize that by not telling you the honest truth, they are robbing you of the opportunity to reach your full potential. These mentors have your best interest in mind because they want to see you succeed instead of being a "yes person."

Choose Mentors with Open-Door Policies.

Everything prior to this moment is great, but if you do not have access to the mentor, then it is in vain. This does not mean that if your mentor is unavailable a couple of times that it's bad, but if your mentor is so busy and it takes several months to get in contact with them, then they are probably not someone who needs to be your mentor at that particular moment. You need someone, especially if you are new in a field, who has an open-door policy and who has time to sit and speak with you.

WHAT TO DO WHEN YOU GET A MENTOR

When your mentor gives you things to do after you meet, make sure you do them. Do not waste the mentor's time by asking for advice and help just to not actually do the things they have instructed you to do.

Your mentor is probably very busy and has a lot of responsibilities in their particular field and within their families. Do not add more stress than they are already under. You are a mentee, which means they are not getting paid to help you and they are doing this out of the kindness of their heart. Do not add more problems for them. You should be a stress-less person that they pour information into.

If you are having troubles, talk to a family member or friend to help you through a situation, not the mentor. You might be thinking, *Well isn't the mentor supposed to help me with that?* No! The mentor is there to help you progress in an area, not be your counselor.

You might not have the money to help that individual, but you should find small ways to show that you appreciate them. If they ask you to babysit their children, make time to do it. If they need a guest speaker for their program, do it. The least you can do is volunteer—without expecting anything in return—to help when asked.

If you are going to have a mentor, use it as motivation and make sure that you succeed. There is no worse feeling in the world than to take time out of your schedule to help someone, and they don't use the advice, put forth effort, or succeed. Make your mentor proud and be great!

Mentors are not permanent. At some point, a mentor should stop helping you with every single project. You should use what they have taught you and spread your wings yourself. You can definitely keep a relationship with your mentors, but you should not use them as a crutch for topics you should be able to address. One day, hopefully, you will become a mentor for someone else.

ACKNOWLEDGMENTS

There are so many people to thank for assisting me in writing this book. This book started as a great idea and turned into something beyond my wildest dreams. I should start by saying that I thank my Lord and Savior Jesus Christ for the inspiration, wisdom, and strength to persist in this journey. If anyone reading this book felt a push inside yourself, or if you have biblical questions, I would love to speak with you. Please reach out at Elevate2Elevate.com.

Next, I have to thank my tremendous editor and formatter Amber for using her expertise to make my vision for the book a reality. She deserves so much of the credit for you reading this book. If you have a book idea, please reach out to her at RootedinWriting.com or to my team at Elevate 2 Elevate to help you make it a reality.

My wife Allie (she probably should've been second—y'all don't tell on me!) would not let me get through this book without me saying her name. She continually supported me and took the time to learn how to create a book cover that turned out amazing! I love you, Baby.

I would be remiss if I didn't give a shout out to my brother, Jamal Gaines; dad, Fred Gaines; and mom, Sonya Gaines. They were and will always be responsible for everything I do because they show me unconditional love. For that I am forever grateful.

Allie and I would also like to thank her parents, the Cook family, for their prayers, encouraging words, and input. You are valued.

I have to say thank you to Jeremy Trojacek, Tony Miller, Jr., my dad, Pastor Chris Edwards, Jerry Willis, and the many, many people who took the time to provide their input on different elements of this book.

Finally, I'd like to thank the countless mentors I've had over the years. There are way too many to count, and I will definitely leave important names out, but I'm thankful and pray continual blessings on your life. This wouldn't be possible without you.

Made in the USA
Middletown, DE
07 May 2021

38646448R00071